Image credit: The Edwin Dawes Collection

Fairy Tales have been around for hundreds of years and are built on the imagination that reaches far into the realms of fantasy. They are tales of right and wrong, of good versus evil. Greed, wickedness, and cruelty are always punished, while kindness, honesty and hard work are rewarded. Fairy Tales are stories of contrasts: heroes and villains, poverty and riches, despair and hope, adversity and triumph. There are recurring motifs too: cunning and cleverness, journeys to distant lands, mysterious travellers, overcoming impossible odds, and of course, not forgetting transformation and magic.

I've always thought that the best stories begin with "Once Upon a Time". That phrase always manages to conjure up an image of an exciting adventure about to begin. An adventure set in a land far away and in a distant time will most definitely have heroes and villains. Perhaps an adventure that draws us into a tangled web of lies and deceit. Perhaps a quest where the intrepid hero has to face monsters and dragons. Perhaps it's a story of humble beginnings, with some wrong turns and bad decisions but comes good in the end, a story filled with excitement and daring and some sadness too. Is there love and romance, keeping readers hopeful of a happy ever after ending? And what of the hero? Is the hero brave and bold, honourable and honest with a true heart? Perhaps this will be an adventure filled with magic, mystery and secrets…

This story has all of the above, including the bit about the dragon, dragon's blood, to be exact. There is even a monster, a real, live graveyard monster. And there are palaces too, shiny, sparkly ones. But this story isn't a Fairy Tale or make-believe. This tale is a true story. It does not start with Once Upon a Time. It starts with a small boy called Samuel.

CONTENTS

CHAPTER ONE

AND SO, THE SHOW BEGINS

Samuel John Rendell was born on 5 November 1860, in Maiden Newton in Dorset. He was baptised in the parish church of St Mary in Powerstock on Boxing Day 1860. He was the eldest of nine children born to Sarah Green and John Thomas Rendell, a local blacksmith. There was something unusual about the marriage of Samuel's parents, as the bride, groom and witness signatures or "marks" are all missing from the document. The only signature on the marriage certificate is that of the minister, the Reverend Thomas Sanctuary. (Thomas Sanctuary went on to become the Archdeacon of Dorset and Canon of Salisbury, so it's difficult to imagine he made such a mistake, or was there some other reason for the lack of signatures?)

(A young Samuel, image credit: Ian Armstrong.)

Samuel's father didn't have the easiest of starts. By age eleven, John Thomas Rendell was an orphan, and as a result, he and his brothers Frederick and William spent time in the Union Workhouse in Beaminster. On leaving the workhouse, all three brothers became blacksmiths in the county of Dorset.
It would be all too easy to conjure up an image of an idyllic rural countryside surrounded by lush fields and fragrant hedgerows. This was, after all, the poetic landscape of Thomas Hardy. But the reality was far grittier and harsher because work wasn't always easy to come by. Supporting a wife and nine children was obviously a priority for John Thomas because he spent his working life moving around Dorset and Somerset wherever he could find work.

And so, Samuel John Rendell spent his first few years living in the tiny village of Frome Vauchurch, which at that time had a population of 171, before moving to the hamlet of Nettlecombe. From there, the family moved to Fordington, a village to the east of Dorchester, and then on to Bournemouth before finally settling in the city of Bath. And it is from Bath that Samuel started his adventure. He had spent a short time as an apprentice blacksmith, but there was obviously something restless and ambitious within him that set him off in a completely different direction. From a very young age, he had been fascinated by all things spiritual, magical and mystical. While his brothers were all content to find work locally, Samuel had other ideas and saw himself as something else entirely. He had big ambitions to become a showman and wasn't afraid to travel the country, selling himself in a variety of guises.

By the 18th century, the city of Bath was a fashionable place to see and be seen. Georgian Bath had become one of the most beautiful spa cities in Europe, and wealthy visitors would flock there to enjoy its restorative waters. Genteel patrons would attend sumptuous balls and supper parties, attend musical performances in elegant drawing rooms and promenade the streets wearing the latest fashions. By the 19th century, the population of Bath had doubled, and like all cities of the time, there was much overcrowding and poverty. Bath began to lose much of its appeal to the upper classes of society. It remained, however, a bustling marketplace, still popular with tourists and less affluent visitors. There were theatre entertainments, travelling shows, music venues, fetes and fairs offering both indoor and outdoor amusements. This was the Bath that Samuel grew up in. After years of moving around for work, Samuel's parents had settled the family in a cottage on Denmark Road. There is census evidence to show that Samuel was working as a blacksmith for a time, no doubt working alongside his father, but that is not where Samuel saw his future.

The travelling entertainment shows caught Samuel's attention. He was fascinated by the side shows where magic tricks were performed and would spend as much time as possible watching the sleight-of-hand illusions. When he was still a young teenager, a travelling minstrel show came to Bath, and Samuel spent so much time watching the conjuring act that he caught the attention of the show's manager. Impressed by Samuel's enthusiasm, the manager offered to take him on as an apprentice conjurer and join the company. Now the question is, did Samuel run away to join the minstrel show, or did he go with his parents' blessing? As part of the company, Samuel would have been expected to take on more than one role or responsibility within the troupe of entertainers. In time, he became an all-round performer, becoming an accomplished musician, singer and actor, as well as learning the art of conjuring. In an interview with The Showman newspaper in 1901, he talks of the time he spent on stage bedaubed with burnt cork as a singing minstrel. Very little is known about Samuel's life as a travelling minstrel, but he would have experienced first-hand precisely what was required to run a successful entertainment company. Those are the years when he would have learned every aspect of stagecraft and developed his performance and audience skills. It is unclear how long Samuel spent travelling the country with the Minstrel Show, but one thing is certain, it's where he perfected his sleight of hand conjuring skills and mastered the art of illusion and magic.
Nothing is known of the minstrel company itself.

(Samuel in minstrel costume, image credit: Ian Armstrong.)

But, during those early years of learning and touring, Samuel encountered many entertainers who were to play significant roles in his future career as a performer. As in modern business practice, back in Samuel's day, it was all about networking, making contacts, building profiles, advertising, branding, and sound marketing strategies. Samuel understood this, and he was a quick learner. Eventually, after completing his apprenticeship, the time came for Samuel to leave the minstrel show. He was passionate and determined to make his name in the entertainment world and wasn't afraid of hard work. It was time for his big adventure to begin. In 1881, at the age of 21, Samuel was living in lodgings in Exeter, working as a banjo player, still using his real name. For the next few years, he was on the road performing to small audiences, gaining experience, expanding his act, and polishing his showmanship skills. In September of the same year, D'Arcs waxwork show came to Samuel's home town of Bath:

FOR A SHORT SEASON ONLY. Commencing this day THURSDAY August 18th 1881.
MONS. D'ARC'S GRAND TABLEAU representing the LAST SUPPER OF OUR LORD, Modelled in wax from the renowned painting of LEONARDO DA VINCI.
The tableau is 25 feet long and the exact size of the painting. It has been patronised by the Royal Family, the Nobility, Gentry and Clergy of this Kingdom and the Continent, and pronounced by the press and Public Opinion a most Wonderful Work of Art.
(Bath Chronicle and Weekly Gazette 18 August 1881.)

The D'Arcs were still exhibiting in Bath two weeks later, having moved their show to the Assembly Rooms. Did Samuel go and see this exhibition? Was he back home visiting his mother while the D'Arcs were in town? There is no evidence to support the theory that Samuel met the D'Arc family this early in his career. However, it isn't beyond the realms of possibility that he did see the exhibition, given that he was a travelling entertainer with the opportunity to return home between engagements or when the work dried up. If he did see the show and meet the D'Arc family, this was an important connection for Samuel, one that was to have serious repercussions in later life.

Samuel began his show business career by performing short musical items and conjuring tricks in private drawing rooms and at Band of Hope concerts around the southwest of England. The Band of Hope was a temperance organisation that was the first national organisation to provide social and recreational events for working-class children. Coffee Taverns opened across the country to raise awareness and encourage abstinence from the demon drink. Public events included a musical programme, usually after the main lecture, which was often illustrated by the use of magic lantern slide shows. Fundraising concerts saw performances by popular artists as well as amateur entertainers. Was Samuel so moved by the suffering and poverty of working-class children that he became an avid supporter of the cause? Or did he simply see the concerts as a means to improving his stagecraft and establishing a reputation for himself?
By 1883, Samuel was a partner in an entertainment company and had begun to use the Rendell Burnette surname.

Ladbrooke and Rendall's Funniosities. This is the title of the entertainment given by a company at Rumsey's Music Hall, High Street, Shepton Mallet, on the first three evenings of this week. The company number about half a dozen and went through a very amusing programme but were not so well patronised as they deserved. The singing of Mr Vere was pleasing in one or two ballads and pathetic songs. Miss Jessie Clyde possesses a nice voice and performed comic and character songs in good style. Mr Edward Coleman was the heavy man of the company, particularly as regards his voice and the buffo songs entrusted to him were given with power. Mr Sam Burnette was a most successful comic and negro delineator, and his impressions were grotesque without descending to vulgarity. Child Maudie, six years old, was introduced and performed a few little parts nicely. The "Black Mashers" was a very amusing negro sketch, and the jokes were evidently enjoyed. Each evening the performance concluded with a comic musical sketch by the whole company.
(Shepton Mallet Journal 31 August 1883)

Although such blatant racism as a form of entertainment is completely abhorrent and unacceptable to us, to Victorian audiences, it was harmless fun. This type of show had arrived in Britain in the1830s from the United States, and by the 1850s, minstrel entertainment was performed in theatres throughout Britain. Victorian minstrelsy depicted the negro as an easy-going carefree character, the opposite of Victorian moral values of self-control. "Blacking up" was considered acceptable entertainment and was seen as much safer than the innuendo and foul language of the music halls.

This was Samuel's first taste of performing in a proper theatrical environment. Rumsey's Music Hall was a step up from performing in drawing rooms and village halls. John Rumsey was an accomplished trumpeter, violinist, teacher, bandmaster and experienced all-round musician. Rumsey had moved to Shepton Mallet in 1850, where he became the music master and organist in the parish church. He opened a music shop that, according to the Shepton Mallet Journal, sold *Harmoniums and Pianofortes from the best London manufacturers.* In 1862, he opened his music hall in Shepton Mallet's High Street, where musical recitals, entertainments and concerts were held. This was Samuel's first taste of performing in a proper theatrical venue.

Samuel was in good company. The Mr De Vere mentioned in the article was Fred De Vere, who began his career as a juvenile actor in theatres around the country. After appearing with Samuel in Shepton Mallet, he went on to form the De Vere and Redford Dramatic Company which toured around Scottish provincial theatres. He subsequently had a successful career as a character actor, appearing in various roles from comedy farces to Shakespearian plays. "The heavy man," Edward Coleman [Colman], was a successful touring actor who enjoyed a long career. In 1903, Coleman and De Vere were to appear together on stage once more at the Lyric, Hammersmith.

RUMSEY'S MUSIC HALL

FUNNIOSITIES

(Jessie Rose Cottle, image credit: Ian Armstrong.)

Throughout those early years on the road, Samuel would visit home as often as he could. It was during one of his visits to Bath that he first met his wife to be. Like many people at the time, Samuel was fascinated by spiritualism, often attending spiritualist meetings wherever he happened to be performing at the time. He would even include it in part of his act in later years. He would often attend spiritualist meetings in various towns, wherever he happened to be performing at the time. During one visit back home to his mother in Bath, Samuel went to a local spiritualist meeting, and it was there he met Jessie Rose Cottle for the first time. Ever the charmer, Samuel struck up a conversation with Jessie Rose, who, according to family sources, found him to be a very polite and attentive young man.

Jessie Rose was one of six children born to William and Ellen Cottle. When she was born, her father was a house painter, and the family was living at Kingsmead Square in Bath. She was christened on the 22nd January 1864, in Trinity parish church in Bath, the same church in which her parents had married in 1849.

Romance blossomed between Samuel and Jessie Rose, and a courtship began. This could not have been easy because Samuel was still trying to establish himself as an entertainer and would have spent much time on the road travelling, accepting engagements across the county. However, in between jobs, he came back home to Bath to visit family and, of course, spend time with Jessie Rose. In January 1884, he and Jessie Rose were married in St Peter's parish church, Twerton. Samuel was still just 23 years old. Their first child, Jessie Emily, was born later that same year and was baptised in the parish church.

For the first few years of their marriage, Samuel and Jessie Rose lived in Kingsmead Terrace, Bath. They seemed to settle into married life, and a second daughter, Hettie Ellen, was born two years later. During these early years of marriage, Samuel was juggling more than one career, working as a blacksmith and a painter to earn money while at the same time following his passion as an entertainer.

CHAPTER TWO
FRANK LIND, DR. LYNN AND PLAGIARISM

(Frank Lind, image credit: June Budd.)

Leaving his wife and two small children at home, Samuel was back on the road. It was during those early years of his stage career that he first met Henry Frank Lind. This may have started as a business relationship, but it grew into a lasting acquaintanceship as their career choices and paths seem to have crossed many times. The fact that both Frank and Samuel shared a common interest in the world of magic and both lived in Bath for a time made it inevitable that they would connect and become friends as well as perform together.

Who was Frank Lind? A larger-than-life character who was undoubtedly a very determined and at times, a single-minded, selfish person. He grasped every available opportunity to advance his career, sometimes with little regard towards others. Henry Frank Lind was born Henry Jesse Warren on March 14, 1856, in Shoreditch. He was the son of a blacksmith and a dressmaker, and his early career as a clerk was unremarkable. However, there seemed to have been a restlessness within him, and from a young age, he was looking for the next best thing.

In 1874, when Frank was working as a commercial traveller, he married Jane Caroline Sharpe in Shoreditch, but life as a salesman around the streets of London obviously didn't feature in Frank's plans. In 1875, his daughter Emmie Caroline was born in Shoreditch, and in January 1876, Frank, Jane and their one-year-old daughter were on a ship bound for Sydney, Australia. Frank continued to work as a commercial traveller, and in April of the following year, Jane gave birth to their son, Henry Jesse Charles Warren, in Sydney. It is unclear how long Frank stayed in Australia with his family, but it couldn't have been very long because, by 1881, he was back in England, living in Hackney and still working as a commercial traveller. But Frank's marriage was in trouble, and it wouldn't last. Frank Lind was known by various names throughout his career, including Dr Lind, Dr Linn, Frank Lynn, Dr Frankland, Professor Lindo, and Henri Garenne.

By 1883, Frank had left his wife and children and was performing as Henri Garenne alongside Madame Garenne in "Pleasant Moments" This was a three-part drawing room entertainment spectacle which offered one or two hours of mirth, music, magic, and mystery. He advertised in various newspapers announcing a tour the following spring to include "marvellous feats and specialities in English and foreign illusions and magic."The most important words in this advertisement are "Madame Garenne" because this was Eliza Agnes Bragger. Eliza was the wife of Luigi Meurice Hiodini (not his real name), another magician. Frank Lind had left his wife and children and had begun a relationship with Eliza. When her marriage with Hiodini ended, Eliza returned to her mother's home in Bishop Auckland. Were both Frank and Eliza staying at her mother's house in Bishop Auckland? "Garenne's" advertisement suggests so. Throughout the following year, Frank travelled around the country performing as Henri Garenne, with Eliza as his stage assistant, Madame Garenne. At the same time, he found time to publish a book, The Art of Modern Conjuring, which other magicians and illusionists dismissed as a blatant act of plagiarism of Professor Hoffman's book, Modern Magic. This didn't do Frank's reputation any good whatsoever, and more trouble was to come.

His wife, Jane Caroline, had filed an action against him on the grounds of desertion. Frank was a wanted man and was being hunted by the police, with numerous adverts placed in the Poor Law Gazette. He was finally caught and appeared in court in November 1884, charged with desertion. All charges were dropped because he was able to talk his way out of the situation and pay all costs thanks to a recent cheque of £20 (around £159 today) for his book. This was a one-off payment because Frank did not return to his wife and children after his court appearance, nor did he support them financially. Instead, he and Eliza continued to perform together all around the country, including an appearance at the London Aquarium, where he committed another act of plagiarism by performing another magician's illusion.

By July of the following year, another warrant for his arrest was issued on the same grounds as before. The police tracked him and Eliza down in Guernsey, where they had been performing for some weeks. When Frank appeared in front of the judge in August 1885, the court heard how his wife and children had been forced into the Workhouse for two months because Frank had not provided for them. The police were able to prove that Frank had been living with another woman in a well-furnished room in Guernsey. Because this wasn't the first time that he had been up on a desertion charge, Frank was sentenced to three months in jail with hard labour. After being released from prison, Frank was back on the stage, and in January 1886, Frank and Samuel got together for the first time – perhaps not the wisest partnership for Samuel.

Around the time of Frank and Samuel's first professional association, there was a well-known and much-respected magician called Dr Lynn who created many of his own illusions. In 1884, Dr Lynn appeared at Crystal Palace with his show:

CRYSTAL PALACE THIS DAY INTERNATIONAL AND UNIVERSAL EXHIBITION
Dr Lynn's New Mystery "Thauma" from 1.00 till 6.30
(London Evening Standard May 7, 1884)

In January 1885, Frank Lind, under the stage name of Henri Garenne, performed Dr Lynn's Thauma at the London Aquarium. Meanwhile, Dr Lynn embarked on a tour around the country with his original Thauma illusion, including an appearance at Samuel's hometown of Bath.

This is most probably where and when Samuel first saw the Thauma illusion. Frank Lind had moved to Bath and was working out of 7 New King Street. By January of the following year, Samuel was the producer of Frank's show. This show was not in any way connected to Dr Lynn's original act. Instead, Frank decided to present his own Thauma illusion show, committing an act of plagiarism and convincing Samuel to act as producer of his show. Plagiarism among magicians and illusionists was fairly common at the time, as few magicians applied for a patent to protect their work due to the financial costs involved. One of the first performances took place in January 1886, in a Bath schoolroom, which was a fundraiser for the parish magazine. Samuel and Frank presented Thauma with the help of Mr Rudge. The Thauma illusion could not be performed without help, and Mr Rudge was just the man to assist Frank. John Rudge was a scientist, lecturer, electrical engineer, scientific instrument maker and inventor. He was familiar with audiences in Bath, often giving displays of his scientific experiments and inventions, including a set of magnetic bagpipes and an electrical fairy light cascade. The Bath Chronicle noted that the audience was small due to bad weather.

While Dr Lynn was able to command audiences at Crystal Palace, Samuel and Frank were reduced to performing in schoolrooms and other low-key establishments. But what exactly was the Thauma mystery?

The showman would open a curtain to reveal a dimly lit alcove with half a lady balancing on a swing. The showman would convince the audience that they were looking at a real human being and, to prove this, would ask the lady several questions, which she would politely answer. To dismiss any idea that mirrors concealed the remaining part of her body, the showman would wave a handkerchief in front, behind and below the lady and then push the swing forwards and sideways, but not backwards. The base of the swing had a gap wide enough for the lady to put her hands through and clasp them beneath her. Then, holding on to a handle on either side of the swing, the wooden base would be removed, leaving the lady suspended. According to The Eastern Evening News, the illusion was clever, leaving the audience with the mystery of how a young woman could exist when her waist was the termination of her body.

Audiences were dwindling, as the novelty of "Thauma" was beginning to lose its appeal to Victorian spectators who were eager for the next outlandish entertainment. Samuel obviously saw how things were going and made the decision to leave Frank Lind's company and strike out on his own yet again. Added to this, there were by now several entertainers with their own "Thauma" show travelling the country, so Lind's company was up against the increasing competition. It was the right decision at the right time because a few months later, Frank Lind placed an advert in The Era trying to sell his entire Thauma props for £5 10s. He also threw in a sword, small conjuring tricks and other apparatus for good measure.

After the disappointment of Thauma, Frank was employed for a short time as stage manager at the Pavilion Theatre in Bath by J.T. Welch, who was the proprietor at the time. This would have provided a steady income for Frank, but it didn't last because of Frank's attitude towards the management. This was a failing in Frank that was to be repeated several times. Frank sent a letter to The Era newspaper complaining that he hadn't been given credit for his hard work in getting the theatre ready for opening. The following week, The Era printed a letter from Fred Fowler, the theatre manager, refuting Frank's claim. The fact that Frank had made his grievances public did not sit well with the owner, so Frank's time as stage manager lasted only a few weeks.

He then embarked upon a new chapter in his career. He produced a handbill advertising his new entertainment, and from that point on, he rarely used the "Henri Garenne" stage name, preferring instead to use either "Dr Frank Lind", "Dr Lind", or simply, "Frank Lind". Eliza Bragger also reinvented herself as "Madame Levaine". The new entertainment was a two-part show, a mixture of sleight of hand conjuring tricks, thought-reading, blood writing and vanishing illusions. Together, Dr Lind and Madame Levaine performed their shows around the UK, including Scotland and Wales, for the next few years. In 1888, he advertised and performed under the names Frank Lind, Dr Lind, Professor Lindo, and Professor Garenne with Madame Levaine as part of each act. In June of that year, they appeared at D'Arc's Waxworks in Cardiff for the first time, by which time Madame Levaine had become the mysterious American lady. In July of the same year, he appeared in Belfast and Dublin, where he called himself the world's greatest mesmerist and claimed his mesmerist show to be the greatest in three kingdoms. Throughout the end of 1889 and the start of 1890, Dr Lind performed in Scotland for several months with a variety show, including his Marvellous Silent Transmission of Thought.

It would be nice to think that although Frank was estranged from his wife, Jane Caroline, he had managed over the years to maintain a relationship with his two children. It's difficult to say what contact he had with Emmie as she was being brought up by Frank's mother, but the 1891 census shows Frank and Eliza on the road with Frank's son. Interestingly, there was another name change as Eliza, Frank and his son, Henry, were all listed with the Warren surname, which implies that Frank and Eliza were husband and wife, but, of course, Frank was still married to Jane, so marriage was impossible.

1891 was an important year for Frank. For the first half of the year, he was still travelling with his conjuring entertainment show and had even dabbled in ventriloquism for a while. In July, he was appointed Manager of Gus Levaine's Royal Albert Theatre in Gloucester. In October of the same year, he became Manager of Gus Levaine's new Variety Hall of Varieties in Cheltenham. So, from a lifetime of being on the road performing his conjuring acts, Frank found himself as manager of not one but two theatres. This must have offered some stability and security for him and Eliza after years of travelling around the country. However, for whatever reason, his employment with Gus Levaine lasted less than six months. In January 1892, Frank placed an advertisement in The Era announcing that he was severing all ties with Levaine's theatres and was available for a new managerial position. One month later, Mr T Owen appointed him as manager of his theatre, The Sydenham Palace in Coventry. This didn't last either, and after just a few months, Frank placed an advert in The Era announcing that he was at liberty with his high-class entertainment, available for halls, piers and galas. Why didn't the management positions work out for Frank? Did he miss the excitement of live performances so much that he went back to the uncertainties of life as a travelling entertainer? Or was it because he was a difficult character and didn't get on with Levaine and Owen, both respected theatre proprietors? It would be interesting to know what Eliza thought of Frank's decision because, at this point, she was pregnant with his child.

VARIETY HALL OF VARIETIES

Frank Inman Lind was born on November 17, 1892, in the village of Escombe, Bishop Auckland. It appears that Eliza returned to her mother's house to have the baby while Frank was on the road performing as Dr Lind and Professor Lindo. Perhaps Frank struggled to secure enough engagements because, in January 1893, he placed adverts looking for work as manager of a music hall or theatre. No offers came in, and whether this was down to Frank's reputation as being a difficult character, it is hard to tell. It wasn't until July 1894 that Eliza re-joined Frank on stage as Madame Levaine, and in March 1895, Dr Lind and Madame Levaine placed an advert in The Era looking for new engagements. By this point, they had included a fast-upside-down sketching cartoon item in their act. For the rest of that year, they completed small engagements around England and in 1897, they appeared at Blackpool's North Pier. In 1898, Frank changed their act and Eliza's stage name to Madame Zilla. They spent most of that year working at Montano's waxwork exhibition show in Sheffield before heading off to Belfast for a three-month engagement at Carter's Waxworks. Whatever changes Frank had made to the act were clearly working, resulting in almost continuous work. He was advertising himself as a scenic tableau expert, and on playbills, Madame Zilla was described as "The Mystic Oracle." After Belfast, they returned to Montano's for a few months and then, in September 1899, Frank became the manager for D'Arc's waxworks no. 2 exhibition in Sheffield, with Madame Zilla as part of the variety show. This managerial position wasn't to last either, and Frank parted company with the D'Arc family just four months later and set up his own travelling waxwork exhibition show. "Madame Lind's Waxworks" opened in Oldham in January 1900. From Oldham, the show moved to Accrington and then on to Llandudno. But unfortunately, it was in Llandudno that things started to go wrong for Frank and Eliza.

On September 10, Madame Zilla appeared in court charged with pretending to tell fortunes using cards. This was a setback for Frank, who was in the process of setting up a new location in Sheffield with a bigger and better show. This would have been an inconvenience for him, but for Eliza, it must have been a devastating experience. The charge she faced came under the Vagrancy Act of George IV, and if proven, she was liable to be treated as a vagabond and a rogue. Unfortunately for Eliza, one of her clients had been William Jones, a Police Inspector with Caernarvonshire Constabulary, and it was he who gave evidence against her in court. If Eliza had proved that she had acted on scientific knowledge in what she said to William Jones or proved that both she and Jones knew it was all pretence and amusement, she would have been found not guilty. However, the prosecution argued that there had been an intention to deceive on Eliza's part. Eliza gave evidence in her defence and claimed that she had practised her art since the age of five and was known as the Lancashire Witch. She explained that after suffering from a seizure, she was unable to continue with her profession as a music hall entertainer, and so she had returned to the business of telling fortunes in order to earn a living. Eliza was found guilty and ordered to pay a fine of £20 plus costs. A week or so after Eliza's court appearance, Madame Lind's Waxworks opened in Sheffield, but less than a month after opening, Eliza became ill and was unable to perform. Frank Placed an advertisement in The Era looking for a replacement for Madame Zilla. Shortly after, he placed another advert thanking people for their letters and telegrams of sympathy, announcing to all that Madame Zilla's case was hopeless, but he had secured Madame Hubert to replace her.

Sadly, Eliza died the same day that Frank's notice appeared in the newspaper. A week after her death, Frank wrote to the North Wales Chronicle claiming that he attributed her death to the shock at being convicted of a crime, and he intended to lodge an appeal with the Home Office for a new hearing.

The death of Eliza was not just a tragedy, but it also had repercussions business-wise for Frank. The business at Sheffield came to nothing, and two months after Eliza's death, Frank appeared at a church fundraiser in Cannard's Grave Room in Shepton Mallet as a ventriloquist and sleight-of-hand entertainer.

Less than six months after Eliza's death, Frank found himself a new "wife". This was Annie Parks (Parkes), born in Aston, Warwickshire and born in New York, USA, depending on which information she chose to give. No marriage record exists for this marriage either, but Frank and Annie started their "married" life in Leeds, where Frank had opened his waxworks in the Kirkgate. By this point, it seems that Frank had very little, if anything, to do with his two children from his first legal marriage, and there is no evidence that they had any contact with their half-sibling, Frank Inman, who was living with Frank and Annie. Frank had secured a management position, and on October 14, 1901, Frank opened the World's Fair in Jarrow, with Lind's Royal Waxworks among the attractions.

After Jarrow, Frank took his waxworks to Spennymoor in County Durham for the festive period, where he also performed his illusion and conjuring entertainment. After Spennymoor, he moved to Consett, and in May 1902, he was called to court to give evidence in another fortune-telling case. He had employed Madame Zarina as a Palmist at his waxworks and explained to the court that he firmly believed in palmistry. Madame Zarina was found guilty with the intent to defraud or deceive, and she was fined £4 plus costs. She was refused extra time to pay because she was considered a flight risk on the grounds that she was using a false name and was here one day and gone the next. This was precisely the same charge that Eliza had faced, two years previously, when she had been fined £20.

In early 1903, Frank's "wife" Annie gave birth to a daughter, Chrissy Mary, who was born in Newcastle, but tragically, Chrissy died soon after she was born. Later that same year, Frank opened his Royal Waxworks at Tynemouth Palace and lost one of his displays in a fire. Unfortunately for him, the local press reported that his whole exhibition had gone up in flames, which resulted in a loss of revenue as the public thought the exhibition was closed.

In early 1904, Annie gave birth to a son, Thomas Frederick, who was born in Durham. After the birth of his son, Frank took his exhibition to Blyth, where disaster struck. Frank had rented an old building that stood between the Liberal Club and the Arcade on Waterloo Road. Around midnight, a fire started in the waxworks, which took hold quickly due to the highly inflammable nature of the exhibition. The fire spread to the northern side of the arcade, and the flames were so intense that soon the southern side caught fire. The fire brigade was powerless to stop the destruction of such an enormous fire that had spread along Waterloo Road. It would have been even worse had barrels of gunpowder from one of the properties not been moved before the fire reached them. In total, fifteen business premises were destroyed at an estimated value of £25,000. Annie narrowly escaped the burning building with the two boys, and she and the baby sustained some injuries as she jumped down a staircase through the dense smoke. A young boy who was helping in the rescue was badly crushed between a piano and a wall and had to be rescued, but luckily, there was no loss of life. Frank's exhibition was destroyed. In fact, he and Annie lost everything apart from the clothes they were wearing on that night. Frank sent a letter to The Era newspaper asking old friends to help him out as he was only partially covered by insurance. A week after the first letter, Frank wrote again asking for financial help from friends and acquaintances, as the only person who had sent any money had been Herbert Crouch of Glasgow. He claimed that the value of everything that he had lost was £520, but he was only insured for £175, and the insurance company were only prepared to pay him £145. It's unclear what the outcome of this situation was, but Frank, Annie and the children were homeless and without means of support.

In 1905, Frank appeared as Professor Lind as part of a concert entertainment at the Assembly Rooms, Old Charleton, Greenwich. Frank's career was definitely in decline, quite possibly as a result of his financial position after the fire at Blyth. By 1911, Frank, Annie and their son, Thomas Frederick, were living in Pontypridd. Both Frank and Annie had become involved in the pseudoscience of character reading. Frank had set himself up as a phrenologist, and Annie was a palmist. After 1911, Frank performed the occasional conjuring act as Professor Lind to small audiences, and then in 1913, Annie gave birth to their second son, John Ernest Lind.

One year later, the story of Frank and Annie took a mysterious turn. On September 2, 1914, Annie left the house with her baby son, John Ernest, boarded a lunchtime train at Aberystwyth, and was never seen again. The Western Mail carried a report of her disappearance and gave a detailed description: "she is described as very thin and delicate with dark brown hair and dark grey eyes, very expressive. Rather bright colour and fallen in cheeks. Scar across bridge of nose. She may be dressed in blue, black, grey, or brown costume, wearing several rings. The baby boy was dressed in white." The relationship must have been in serious trouble for Annie to have taken such drastic action. So, what happened to her? She and Frank had never married, so I suspect she either changed her name or reverted to her maiden name. How long did Frank look for her? Did he ever track her down? One clue came almost a year after Annie's disappearance. Frank placed a wanted advert in a Hampshire newspaper looking for the address of Madame La Roma, lady palmist, with a reward for information. Did this mean that he was simply looking for a new palmist for his business now that he had lost Annie, or did he believe this to be her? By this time, Frank was struggling financially as he had resorted to cleaning and repairing shop fittings and draper's models. In the end, he didn't spend too long looking for Annie because the following year, he married Margaret Lee in Newport Register Office in 1916, and a certificate for this marriage exists. However, the marriage was illegal because Frank was still married to his first wife, Jane Caroline Sharpe and had, therefore, committed an act of bigamy. Somehow, Frank convinced his new wife, Margaret, to be part of his show, and in 1917, he opened a waxwork exhibition in Hastings. In July of that year, both Frank and Margaret appeared in court charged under the vagrancy act on charges of pretending to tell fortunes, the very same offence that Eliza had faced. Unfortunately for them, the two women who gave evidence against them in court were both wives of police officers who had been acting upon instructions to visit the fortune-telling booth. Frank claimed that he didn't tell fortunes but studied people's hands and had been in the business of exhibitions and amusements. Nevertheless, he was found guilty and fined £5 or 25 days imprisonment with a week to pay. Margaret pleaded guilty to a similar charge at another show and was fined £2, 10s.

Frank Lind was not the best of men. It is said that you should never judge a man's actions until you know his motives, and while it would be unfair to judge Frank's behaviour simply because we shall never have all the facts, his actions are the actions of a selfish man. He stole tricks and illusions from other magicians and passed them off as his own. He plagiarised Professor Hoffmann's work in his own book in order to make money. He completely abandoned his wife and children to the Workhouse so that he could continue his affair with Eliza. And, after conversations with descendants of Frank, it transpires that he gave away two of his sons to travelling show people. Frank Inman Lind, Eliza's child and Thomas Frederick Lind, Annie's child, were given to fairground travellers. Is this why Annie walked out on Frank and boarded that train with her baby son? It really is inconceivable that a father could do such a thing, but it left Frank free of family responsibilities and free to commit the act of bigamy with Margaret Lee.

On a final note, it is said that history repeats itself, and in the case of Frank's son, Thomas Frederick, that's exactly what happened when he bigamously married a woman in Glasgow. However, unlike his father, he was discovered and convicted of the act of bigamy.

In 1919, Frank Lind died in the County Asylum, Bridgend, Wales.

CHAPTER THREE
FAKE NAMES AND WIZARDRY

(A young Samuel, image credit: Ian Armstrong.)

It must have been around the time of Hettie Ellen's birth that Samuel decided to change his name and assume a professional one. However, one stage name wasn't enough because Samuel had created two very different stage personas for himself. Under the name *Frederick Rendell Burnette,* he was an all-round entertainer, musician, comique, singer and actor. But as *Professor Burnette*, he appeared on stage as a conjurer, magician, legerdemain, mind reader, ventriloquist and mesmerist.

In 1886, after parting company from Frank Lind, Samuel secured an engagement with Harry Williams, a musical agent based in Bath who was producing a Grande Fete at Cranmore Hall for the Wickham Habitation Primrose League.

PROFESSOR BURNETTE
The celebrated Australian Wizard in his clever entertainment of magic and mystery, introducing wonderful sleight of hand experiments, thought–reading and mesmerism, and his newest novelty, The Flying Aviary.
(Western Gazette 3 September 1886)

Samuel was obviously a success because he performed throughout September in several more shows for the Primrose League, each time billed as "Professor Burnette, The Australian Wizard." Being known as Professor Burnette was not enough for Samuel, and he must have thought that by selling himself as an Australian Wizard made his act more unique and exotic. After all, there couldn't have been that many Australian Wizards in Bath at the time! But did he perform his magic tricks with an Australian accent? Two months later, Samuel appeared at the International Bazaar in the Assembly Rooms in Bath with a new show:

The Programme includes Galatea, the Greek Mystery and other feats of illusion worked by
Professor Burnette and Mr Lavis.
(Bath Chronicle and Weekly Gazette 18 November 1886)

Mr Lavis was William Lavis, the son of a commercial clerk, who was born in Rotherhithe and began his career as a heraldic artist and decorator. He became involved in amateur dramatic shows around the Bath area as a scenic artist and prop maker. Samuel would have easily convinced William to assist with the show because they were neighbours and possibly friends, both living on Kingsmead Street in Bath.

It is clear that Samuel wasn't just perfecting his stage skills, he was a clever salesman and knew exactly how to market and sell himself as a showman. It is one thing to embark upon a musical career, performing to small local audiences, constantly facing criticism and knockbacks, and chasing down the next paying job while still having to pay the rent and raise a family. But Samuel was doing more than that. He had created two completely different stage acts for himself, proving his versatility as an entertainer. He was astute enough to realise there were wider audiences and bigger opportunities to embrace. And, like his father before him, that is precisely what he did. Samuel went wherever the work was, building up his reputation and making himself known in the show business world.

Intriguingly, Frank Lind had appeared at the same Assembly Rooms just a few weeks before with his sensational and mystical two-part entertainment show entitled World Of Wonders And Enchantment, including the great Parisian sensation, "The Instantaneous Disappearance Of A Lady". At the time, Frank was living at New King Street in Bath, a few streets away from Samuel's house, so the two were probably still in contact with each other.

Shortly after presenting his Greek Mystery, Galatea in Bath, Samuel took his show to the Royal Aquarium Theatre in Westminster, London. He used his appearance there as a clever marketing ploy because from then onwards, he advertised his show as the "Original Royal Aquarium Galatea". Using the word "royal" on a playbill would have added a touch of class to attract audiences in provincial theatres. This was the show that he took to Glasgow. At the same time that Samuel was performing his show in Glasgow, another entertainer called Harry Addison was performing it at the Royal Aquarium in London:

WANTED. Partner with about £10 to join Harry Addison, now performing with great success,
Royal Aquarium Galatea show and the wonderful Mechanical Hand. Address Harry Addison,
Royal Aquarium, Westminster or 10 Roehampton Street, Vauxhall Bridge Road, London.
(The Era 12 January 1887)

Harry Addison had performed with the renowned G.A. Farini and P.T. Barnum. He was an inventor and performer of illusions on a relatively grand scale and exhibited his freak show for more than twenty years at the London Aquarium. He was the inventor and creator of "Barnumia", which was a collection of slides representing the various "freaks" who, at some point, had been exhibited.

With the help of a lantern, the slides were projected onto a screen. The slide show lasted twenty minutes, with Addison describing the life history of sixty subjects. Samuel appeared at the London Aquarium during the time that Addison was performing, and he would have witnessed his illusions firsthand. Later, in 1891, Samuel travelled around the country with a new show, "The Living Mermaid", which was another of Addison's illusions. This was another blatant example of plagiarism, which was rife among magicians at the time.

Victorian fascination with science, exploration and foreign cultures prompted naturalists to scour the world in search of exotic animals, which they exhibited as "a cabinet of curiosities". This was extended to include humans who were perceived to have physical differences, and so the "freak show' was born. Promotors claimed that people with exceptional bodies faced a life of poverty, and they were merely providing employment, which allowed them to lead more fulfilling lives. It was, of course, outrageous exploitation by the promotors. However, this eased the conscience of audiences to accept and support such shows, believing that it was done with the consent of those on display. The historian and journalist Henry Mayhew was vehemently against such shows, describing them as "nothing more than moral corruption and human degradation." Thankfully, the fascination of human differences as a form of entertainment dwindled as the public began to accept Mayhew's way of thinking by questioning the moral and ethical values of these shows.

CHAPTER FOUR

A FIRST TASTE OF GLASGOW

In 1887, Samuel went to Glasgow, where he secured an engagement with Cornelius Coupe Fell at the Trongate. C. C Fell claimed that his waxwork exhibition and museum was the brightest and smartest attraction of its kind outside of London.

Cornelius Coupe Fell was born in Blackburn, Lancashire, about 1844, the son of a cotton manufacturer. His early career as a clerk and a bookkeeper was uneventful, but at the same time, he was establishing a second career for himself as an exhibition proprietor. In 1880, he sold off all the props and models in his mechanical exhibition, including scenery and staging. This was just before his move to Glasgow, where he set up his waxwork exhibition and entertainment business at 101 Trongate. By the time Samuel arrived in Glasgow, C. C. Fell's American Waxworks had claimed to have been in business for about twenty years. However, the 1861, 1871 and 1881 census documents all prove that C.C. Fell was still living in Blackburn as a bookkeeper and was definitely not at the Trongate until sometime after 1881. C.C. Fell's was more than just a waxworks exhibition hall. A newspaper article from 1897 mentions that Mr Fell had been proprietor at the Trongate for fifteen years, which places the opening of Fell's to around 1882 rather than the 1866 date claimed in advertisements. Fell's was more than just an exhibition space for wax models. It was a complete entertainment venue for visiting variety and "freak" shows that were popular at the time:

> *"Wanted for Fell's Waxworks and Exhibition established twenty years at 101 Trongate, Glasgow. Attractive in and out Living Novelties, Human or Animal Freaks of Nature, Theatre of Arts Marionettes or anything really sensational for immediate and future dates."*
> *(The Era, 10 April 1886)*

> *Wanted for Fell's Waxworks and American Museum, 101 Trongate, Glasgow (Established 1806) Freaks and Attractions that can be featured for several open dates. Special engagement of Castagna, the French Living Skeleton.*
> *(The Era, 10 August 1901)*

Samuel would probably have been expected to perform two shows daily to tough, opinionated, vocal audiences who were at best raucous and, at worst, intoxicated and not averse to throwing assorted missiles on stage if they disliked the act. Nevertheless, Samuel was a success with the Glasgow audiences because his original short engagement was extended for six weeks:

> *Wanted by Professor Burnette, T T Engagements for his Original Royal Aquarium "Galatea" and other Sensational Wonders. Still appearing with Gigantic success at Fell's Waxworks Exhibition, 101 Trongate Glasgow. Good Boss. Thanks.*
> *(The Era 12 February 1887)*
> *Wanted for Fell's Waxworks and Variety Exhibition, 101 Trongate Glasgow, Living novelties and other attractions. Professor Burnette and Madame Hilda, Illusionists finish tonight six weeks successful engagement.*
> *(The Era 12 March 1887)*

At that time, The Trongate and Argyle Street must have been an assault on Samuel's senses. Singing saloons entertained thousands every night, where the entertainment consisted of comedians, comic singers, comic dancers and every variety of minstrelsy. MacLeod's Waxworks and Fell's Waxworks were at The Trongate, alongside The Britannia Music Hall, while Crouch's Superior Waxworks Exhibition was on Argyle Street. Samuel made a lasting impression on C. C Fell:

Professor Burnette The Modern Magician gave universal satisfaction to large and appreciative audiences. I consider him to be a clever sleight of hand performer and his performance is novel, pleasing and entirely devoid of any vulgarity.
Signed Cornelius C Fell, Proprietor, American Novelty Palace, 101 Trongate Glasgow
(From Samuel's own collection of testimonials, 1886)

However, the same year that Samuel made his first appearance in Glasgow, C. C. Fell was summoned to court by the Procurator Fiscal. Much interest was taken in the case for two reasons: Firstly, to test the relevancy of an Act of Parliament, and secondly, the accused was a well-known businessman who was highly respected in the city of Glasgow. According to The Era newspaper, he was charged with having carried out his business as a waxwork's proprietor " in such a manner as to be an annoyance to the neighbourhood and inhabitants of the Trongate." C.C. Fell had dared to play an organ and allowed people to congregate and shout at the door of his premises. This was apparently contrary to section 247, article 3 of the Glasgow Improvement Act 1866. Fell's solicitor argued that the charges under that section of the act, known as the Sanitary Nuisance Act, did not apply as it was only intended to deal with behaviour which might be injurious to health. The Procurator Fiscal argued that playing an organ was a nuisance and "offensive to the ears of the tradesmen who carried on business in the immediate neighbourhood." The case was dismissed.

Over the years, the Trongate became a thriving, popular and successful enterprise. In 1897, C.C. Fell expanded his business by opening a new waxworks exhibition shop at the Victoria Rooms in Hull. He continued to run his show at The Trongate until 1904, when he sold it for four hundred and thirty-seven pounds, ten shillings, to the eccentric English entrepreneur Albert Ernest Pickard. C.C. Fell died in 1907, barely three years after retiring from the Trongate. His obituary in The Era stated that "he was one of the most courteous gentlemen who was kind and affable to all and a more intelligent gentleman than is generally found in ordinary commercial circles and was, in every respect, a credit to the city of Glasgow." A.E Pickard continued to run the venue as a waxwork's variety show, claiming:

> *"Pickard's Museum and Zoo, 101 Trongate. Over one million novelties. All the world in wax. Open all day."*

In 1906, Pickard bought the Britannia Music Hall, just two doors down from his waxwork museum. Before undergoing extensive refurbishment, the Britannia had a certain reputation. There were three Ps associated with the venue: Pee – there was no toilet in the theatre until 1893, and audience members would avail themselves of any corner or wall inside the building. Poo – patrons often brought horse droppings in with them to hurl on stage if they didn't like the act. Prostitutes – one particular corner of the balcony was known to be where most business transactions occurred, the number of men's trouser buttons found in this location providing the evidence!

GALATEA AND OTHER SENSATIONAL WONDERS

CHAPTER FIVE

PROFESSOR BURNETTE, PROFESSOR HOFFMANN AND A NIGHT IN WONDERLAND

After the Trongate, Samuel secured a three-week run at Gambart's in Leeds before moving on to perform in Blackburn.

> *Wanted by Professor Burnette and Madame Hilda, dates for their Royal Aquarium Galatea and Sensational Wonders. Good Shop: on sharing terms only. Splendid pictures, own Doorsman. Address Blackburn Post Office. Three weeks at Gambart's Leeds.*
> (The Era 16 April 1887)
> *Wanted. Good shop on sharing terms for Professor Burnette's Royal Aquarium Galatea and Sensational Wonders. 19 Barton Street, Blackburn.*
> (The Era 23 April 1887)

Gambart's Novelty Palace, managed by Ernest Gambart Baines, was an exhibition hall that attracted various travelling, temporary acts, including Whatman's Lilliputian Marionettes, Professor Sirron, the Crystal Palace Conjuror and Will le Claire, Comical Conjuror. After Glasgow and Leeds, Samuel returned to Bath, where he continued to perform around the southwest region as *Professor Burnette*, developing and producing new conjuring shows that he performed before relatively large audiences as well as much smaller provincial audiences. In July 1887, he appeared at the Pavilion Theatre in Bath, which was at that time under the management of Harry Williams, who had previously employed Samuel for the Primrose League Fetes.

> *"I have very great pleasure in specially recommending the exceedingly clever and amusing conjuring performance of Professor F Burnette. It has been my good fortune to engage him on many occasions and he has always given the most perfect and genuine satisfaction to very large audiences. He has a pleasing manner and address and can always be relied upon to carry out his engagements successfully."*
> *H. Williams, Manager Pavilion and Principal Fete and Gala Caterer for West of England.*
> (From Samuel's own collection of testimonials, 1887)

Harry Williams, the son of an accountant and music teacher, was born in Bristol and settled in Bath, where he set up his wine and spirit business. For a while, he was also the agent for Bristol United Breweries and the local representative for the Lamb Brewery in Frome. However, he was a man of many interests, which included all things musical and theatrical. He was an agent and organiser for local fetes, concerts, charity events, and boxing matches around the western counties of England. For fourteen years, he was the chairman and manager of the Bath Music Hall, which became the Pavilion and then the Lyric Theatre. It is on record that when he was manager of the Pavilion, he once refused to engage Harry Lauder because he asked for £1 more than the going rate for that theatre at that time. Later that same year, Samuel had a small role performing during the interval for The United Patriots Benefit Society in the Guildhall in Bath:

> *...the room was crowded to excess and the applause was hearty and prolonged. The unseemly behaviour of one portion of the audience who persisted in interrupting one singer should not go unnoticed. In the interval, Professor Burnette gave a capital conjuring performance, the various items of which were enthusiastically received by the spectators.*
> (Bath Chronicle and Weekly Gazette 6 October 1887)

After his appearance at the Guildhall, Samuel was signed up by the London Entertainment Company. This was an agency working out of 31 Oxford Street, which had a variety of artistes for every occasion:

WANTED by the Manager London Entertainment Co, 31 Oxford Street W, Ventriloquists and Dissolving Views. We only advertise for what we do require. I beg to state what I have often mentioned in letters, so–called Second Sight is not a success in the Nobility's Drawing Rooms. Their intelligence enables them to detect the manipulation of words or code. Such rudeness as the Flannel Petticoat, Flat Iron and Pawn Ticket Dodge would not be tolerated...
(The Era 2 January 1886)

(Handbill illustration, image credit: Peter Lane Collection.)

Prof. F Burnette WONDER WORKER

Thought Reader and Illusionist
Has much pleasure in announcing that he has made arrangements with The London Entertainment Company, 31 Oxford Street, W.
To supply all kinds of entertainments especially adapted for Christmas and Evening Parties, Church Schools, Temperance, Band of Hope and other Societies, Bazaars, Soirees, Concerts and Charity Institutions.
Conjuring, Illusionary, Second Sight, Thought Reading, Ventriloquial Punch and Judy, Light and Dark Seances, Musical and Refined Negro Performances.
Charities readily assisted.
For Present Season 1887 – 1888:
Professor Burnette can supply new, novel and refined Drawing Room Entertainment of Natural Magic entitled World of Wonder including chaste, modern amusing illusions and feats of dexterity with beautifully expensive and mysterious apparatus, never before seen, accompanied by ZANO the Wonderful Automaton figure.
(Printed publicity handbill 1887 by R. Rogers, Bristol)

Samuel had these handbills produced so that he could advertise and promote his entertainments. It would be interesting to know how many he had printed, as in 1886, 5000 copies would have cost him just over six shillings. The average annual male wage back in 1885 was around £46. Samuel also had a programme printed that gave a more detailed outline of his three-part show. Part one was entitled "Parisian Wonders, A Night in Wonderland", which was the conjuring and sleight of hand entertainment. Part two was "Thought Transference and Thought Reading Extraordinaire" by Miss Hilda Nelson, including Cabinet of Mystery or "At the Stake". Finally, "Merry Moments" concluded the show with a variety of minstrel, musical and comedy numbers. Professor Edwin Dawes wrote about Samuel's act in his column, *A Rich Cabinet of Magical Curiosities,* originally published in *The Magic Circular*. Referring to Samuel's three-part show, he says:

> "... Parisian wonders A Night in Wonderland embraced a selection of conjuring feats which from their titles seem to have been pretty standard for the period and depended heavily on Hoffmann."

Professor Hoffmann was Angelo John Lewis, a barrister and professor of law, and he was someone that I believe Samuel knew very well, although it was unlikely that they ever met. Like Samuel, Angelo John Lewis loved all things magical. To avoid embarrassment within legal circles, Mr Lewis wrote under the name Professor Hoffmann. He became an established authority and accomplished author on magic, puzzles, games, illusions and entertainments of the time. He began his writing career with a series of 48 articles on magic for boys, which were published in the magazine *Every Boy's Annual*. The articles were then published in one volume, *Modern Magic,* in 1876. Of all the books he wrote, "Modern Magic" is perhaps the most famous and well-read.

It is more than likely that Samuel read every article written by Professor Hoffmann and would have devoted himself to perfecting every trick and following his advice. The articles were, in fact, a magician's manual, advising on staging, appearance, props, dress code, routines and interaction with the audience. Other chapters give detailed instructions for various conjuring and sleight-of-hand tricks, while others explain larger stage illusions and effects. Hoffmann also wrote on the use of automated mechanical models and marionettes and stated that success relied upon the credulity and ignorance of the audience as much as the perfection of the trick itself. The final chapters in Hoffmann's *Modern Magic* deal with spiritualism and clairvoyance, arguing that people who believed in such things was simply further proof that there were no bounds to human stupidity and ignorance. Samuel's future career as both a magician and an independent businessman is proof that he was a devoted reader and student of Hoffmann: he would include the use of both waxwork marionettes and mechanical models and go on to embrace new technology in his ventures.
"Never tell your audience beforehand what you are going to do."
(Professor Hoffmann, Modern Magic.)

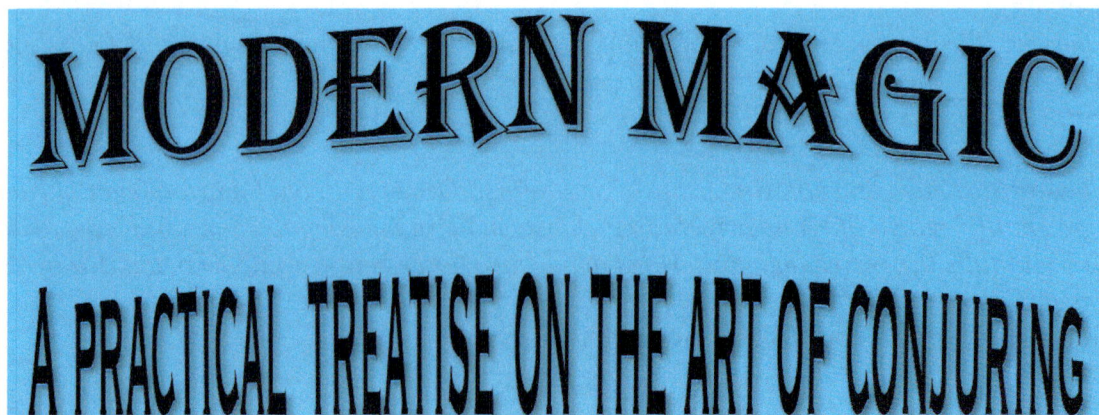

PROFESSOR F. BURNETTE

(From the Royal Aquarium, London)

— PROGRAMME. —

IN THREE PARTS.

Part I.

PARISIAN WONDERS!

A NIGHT IN WONDERLAND.

Professor BURNETTE'S Programme of Entirely New Feats selected from the following:—

Introduction to Wonderland—The Crystal Casket and Enchanted Balls—Flora's Fairy Garden, or Something from Nothing—The Pastry Cook; or, The Curious Travels and Adventures of a Wedding Ring, introducing BURNETTE's Trained Birds—The Phantom Cage, or where is it?—Obedient Cards and Marvellous Sword Feat—Grandma's Enchanted Frame, or the new way to Mend Crockery—Extraordinary Illusion with a Borrowed Watch—Sleight-of-Hand Feats with Real Eggs—The Wonderful Flight of Marked Money—The Great Hindoo Water Feat: The First Lesson—A Charming Arrival: Please Treat me as One of the Family—The Mutilated Handkerchief and Laughable Mistake—The Glass of Water endowed with Life—The Knotty Question—The Magic Fruit—Sword of Mystery—Sleight-of-Hand Experiment with Real Egg and Borrowed Handkerchief—The Vanishing Bouquet of Flowers—The Crystal Treasury—Mystic Roses and Paper Cone—BURNETTE's Aquarium—Don't Use your Hat for Shopping: Showing how to convert a 6d into a Bank, a Bazaar, a Wardrobe, and Co-operative Stores.

Part II.

✠ Thought-Transference and Thought-Reading Extraordinary ✠

BY

MISS HILDA NELSON.

Pronounced by the London Press to be the most incomprehensible mystery now before the public.

"The lady was successful in all the experiments."—*Literary World.*

(Playbill, image credit: Peter Lane Collection.)

Has the honour to announce that he will introduce, as above, his unequalled Magical, Illusory, Mesmerical, Humorous, Musical, and Sensational Melange,

"PARISIAN WONDERS,"

Introducing the latest Parisian Novelties, replete with the Superb, Elegant, and Mystic. Pronounced by crowded audiences TO BE SOMETHING NEW.

| Front Seats, | ; Second Seats, | ; Third Seats, | . |

Doors open at 7.30; commence at 8.

(Playbill, image credit: Peter Lane Collection.)

CHAPTER SIX

THE MAGICIAN'S ASSISTANT

Throughout 1888, Samuel performed in shows such as *Professor Burnette's Parisian Wonders, She at the Stake, Covent Garden, and The Cabinet of Mystery*. He was often billed as a conjurer and mesmerist as well as a thought reader. He was a regular performer at the Assembly Rooms in Weston Super Mare, often performing as both *Frederick Burnette* and *Professor Burnette* in the same show:

> *"Professor Burnette kept the audience highly entertained for nearly half an hour with his Cabinet of Mystery and She*
> *at the Stake in which the assistance of several members of the audience was requisitioned. He successfully exposed*
> *so called "spiritualism" and was loudly applauded. Mr F Burnette performed a bones solo which found favour with*
> *the audience. A comic negro sketch by Mr F Burnette introducing a banjo solo and a ballad with chorus, preceded*
> *the National Anthem."*
> (Weston Super Mare Gazette 21 November 1888)

Early in his career, Samuel established a working relationship with Hilda Neilson. (Also known as Hilda Nelson.) Hilda was a mezzo-soprano, and together they appeared in concerts across England and Wales. Hilda was also "Madame Hilda", appearing alongside Professor Burnette as his magician's assistant.

> *The programme consisted of songs ably rendered by Miss Hilda Neilson and Mr F Burnette comique recitations. A special attraction was Professor F Burnette in a conjuring entertainment entitled "Parisian Wonders" and a pretty experiment called, "Covent Garden".*
> (Weston Mercury 20 October 1888)

> *At Woodborough Hall Winscombe, the programme consisted of songs ably rendered by Miss Hilda Neilson, (mezzo-soprano) and Mr F Burnette, (comique recitations, pathetic and humorous) Professor F Burnette, (thought reading séance)*
> (Weston Super Mare Gazette 27 October 1888)

> *The evening's programme gave great satisfaction: bones solo and original comic sketch by Mr F Burnette. The comic sketch, introducing stump speech, "The Vacant Chair", "The Old Folk at Home" and "Razors in the Air" by Mr F Burnette and Miss Hilda Neilson.*
> (Weston Super Mare Gazette 22 December 1888)

At some point, Hilda changed her stage name to "Marie Neilson" and continued to perform with Samuel. (Not to be confused with another Marie Neilson, a famous Shakespearian actress who toured Australia and New Zealand before returning to a successful career on the London stage.)

> *Wanted. Known. Big Success. Mr Burnette, the World's Mystery and Miss Marie Neilson, Fletcher's Bazaar, Newport, disengaged shortly.*
> (The Era 21 February 1891)

> *Wanted. Known. Mr Burnette and Marie Neilson, Sensational wonder Workers, third week comfortable engagement with Madame Fletcher's Bazaar, Swansea. Disengaged shortly.*
> (The Era 7 March 1891)

Wanted, Known. Fred Burnette and Miss Marie Neilson, big success, Victoria Hall, Cheltenham. Thanks to Shakespeare Shenton Esq, two weeks comfortable engagement. Wanted, Halls, seaside. Address above.
(The Era 27 June 1891)

"She at the Stake" was one of Samuel's better known, more popular acts:

> *She at the Stake proved an attractive item and quite a mysterious mystery.*
> *"She", (Miss Marie Neilson) is described as "the sensation of London, the rage of Paris and the wonder of the 19th Century" introduced by Professor F Burnette from the Royal Aquarium, was bound hand and foot to a stake (in the presence of and by a local committee), and was placed into a cabinet in which she could be heard playing a tambourine and ringing some bells. Whilst bound, "She" also cut a pretty pattern out of some tissue paper, made a cigarette, struck a match and when the curtain was drawn back was seen smoking. A watch was then borrowed and placed in the pocket of a committee member who took a seat in the cabinet next to the bound woman. At that moment, the pianist on seeing the hesitation of the committee member, who had a sense of humour, began playing the Dead March in Saul. As everyone expected, when the pair were once more exposed to view, "She" had the watch and the local man was mystified as to how it had left his pocket."*
> (The Citizen 12 August 1891)

The "She At The Stake" illusion had been performed by Lieutenant Albini (real name Frederick Baxter Ewing) and his assistant, Marie Gautier, several years before Samuel and Hilda performed their version. Dressed in a military-style uniform, Albini was variously described as The Marvellous Thought Reader, Modern Deceptionist, and the Talented Royal Humourist. Albini was also connected to The London Entertainment Company, the same agency which had employed Samuel. James Lathbury Tanner and Frederick Ewing were the partners behind The London Entertainment Company, and it is highly likely that Frederick Ewing and Frederick Baxter Ewing were the same person. The illusion continued to be performed by numerous magicians around the country for many years. As late as 1914, a Mr Levard performed it at The Grand Theatre, Aberaman, Wales, and offered £50 reward to anyone who could prove that he used any traps or duplicate assistants in his illusion.

Samuel and Hilda/Marie continued to perform together for many years until they parted company, with Samuel becoming more diverse in his ventures while Marie went on to pursue her musical career by performing in variety and musical acts for many years.

CHAPTER SEVEN

PROFESSOR QUISTO AND TEDDY FLETCHER

Samuel and Jessie welcomed their first son, Victor Burnette, who was baptised in Twerton parish church in January 1888. On the baptism record, Samuel is listed as a musician. Unfortunately, tragedy was to follow as Samuel's daughter, Hettie Ellen, died in early 1888, aged just one year old. A fourth child, Marie, was born in 1889 and baptised in Roadhill parish church, Wiltshire. On Marie Dorothy's baptism record, Samuel is listed as a Professor of Legerdemain. Sadly, Marie Dorothy died in 1890, just three months after her birth. In 1890, the infant mortality rate was 150.7. in every thousand. One year later, another daughter, Grace Mona, was born and baptised in Twerton parish. On the baptism entry, Samuel is simply listed as a Professional. During these years, Samuel was still travelling around Somerset, Wiltshire, Dorset, Gloucestershire and Wales, performing his conjuring shows wherever he could find the work. This meant accepting engagements in venues both large and small.

> *...a large and appreciative audience gathered at the Kiosk, Knightstone...Professor Burnette, conjuring and songs.*
> (Weston Super Mare Gazette 19 September 1888)

> *...appearing at the Victoria Hall, Weston Super Mare, Professor F Burnette, Thought Reader, Mesmerist and Presdigitateur.*
> (Weston Super Mare Gazette 20 October 1888)

> *Professor Burnette gave a very clever entertainment at the National schoolroom in Bruton on Thursday evening.*
> (Bristol Mercury 19 October 1889)

> *Lady Paget provided a treat for the children in their schoolroom in the shape of a good tea and a conjuring entertainment by Professor Burnette who has visited the neighbourhood several times before.*
> (Shepton Mallet Journal 17 January 1890)

In February 1890, Samuel appeared in a variety show held at the Malden Wanderers Cricket Club. He was appearing as the musical entertainment, billed as Mr Rendell and not as Professor Burnette. This was when Samuel first met Professor Arthur Quisto, a ventriloquist and puppet maker who used life-size models in his act. (This is not to be confused with Arthur Quisto, whose real name was Edwin Simms, 1882 – 1960, and who was also a ventriloquist and puppet creator.)

This Professor Quisto was born around 1865 in Oxford and considered himself an actor, comedian, singer, musician, and ventriloquist. He established his own entertainment business, Quisto's Crystal Palace Combination Company, to include various acts that toured around the country. Quisto was clearly impressed with Samuel's talents because, by September 1890, he had become part of Quisto's touring show:

> *Wanted. Known Mr Burnette, Royal Presdigitateur, with his Sensational Entertainment, Parisian Wonders on tour with Quisto's Crystal Palace Company.*
> (The Era 20 September 1890)

The timing of this must have been a welcome source of income for Samuel because Quisto was about to embark on a sixteen-week tour of the provinces. Just at the time when Samuel joined the company, Quisto had advertised for a Baggage Man to join the company at once for the tour. He was also looking for a "Good lady solo pianist to join his Ventriloquial and Concert Company." The successful applicant had to dress well on and off the stage and send a photo to the post office at Whitney, Oxon. However, Samuel wasn't content to simply appear as part of Quisto's show because by October of 1890, he had taken on a more significant responsibility with the company:

A REFINED DRAWING ROOM ENTERTAINMENT
TOWN HALL CHIPPING NORTON
TWO NIGHTS ONLY
Quisto's Crystal Palace Combination Company. Ventriloquism. Voices here, voices there, voices everywhere. London Street Cries! Funny Folks! Eight Life Size Automata! Parisian wonders including The Mystic Hand. The Crystal Palace Mystery, THAUMA. Vocal and instrumental solos. The beautiful Ines, the Ariel Wonder. She At The Stake!
The whole comprising two hours refined yet mystifying and amusing entertainment. Elaborate stage fittings and appointments.
Business Manager, Mr F R Burnette.
Stage Manager, Mr A J Butler.
Agent in Advance, Mr D'Vaine.
Sole Proprietor, Mr Arthur Quisto.
(Oxfordshire Weekly News 15 October 1890)

Looking at the list of entertainments, it is interesting to see Thauma as part of the programme, but there is no indication of who was performing it. Samuel was undoubtedly familiar with the illusion as he had produced Frank Lind's Thuama years earlier, so it could easily have been him. Arthur Quisto continued to appear in variety shows across the country for many years with his ventriloquist act of life-size marionettes.

After Quisto's, Samuel had such a passion and a need to perform that he accepted work wherever he could, mindful of the fact that he had a wife and three young children to support, with another child on the way. He secured a position with Teddy Fletcher at the Empire Palace of Varieties in Newport, Gwent. Edward Fletcher and his wife, Angelina, were travelling showpeople who exhibited their waxwork model sideshows around the country. They also had established permanent waxwork venues in Newport and Swansea, which had indoor theatres for visiting entertainers. This was an important engagement for Samuel because Edward Fletcher was a well-established showman and exhibitor. (Not to be confused with Edward Fletcher, manager of the Theatre Royal in Cardiff.) So important, in fact, that Samuel bought himself a new dress suit and travelled to Newport to present himself at the Theatre. The "Palace" was a particular disappointment for Samuel, who had some difficulty in locating it. Instead of a sumptuous theatre, it was, in fact, a small shop with a doorway access on Commercial Road. Nevertheless, although he was disappointed with his venue, Samuel fulfilled his week-long engagement as a conjurer. He presented himself as a very well-spoken, neatly dressed, clever magician and the weekly takings exceeded expectations. Teddy Fletcher was so impressed with him that he extended his run to appear in another of his venues:

Wanted. Known. Big Success. Mr Burnette, the world's Mystery and Miss Marie Neilson, Fletcher's Bazaar, Newport, Disengaged shortly. 32 Charles Street, Newport.
(The Era 21 February 1891)

Wanted. Known. Mr Burnette and Miss Marie Neilson, Sensational Wonder Workers. Third week comfortable engagement Madame Fletcher's Bazaar, Swansea. Disengaged shortly.
(The Era 7 March 1891)

After appearing in Newport and Swansea, Samuel continued to travel around the country performing his Sensational Wonders, She At The Stake and a new act entitled The Living Mermaid. (Lieutenant Albini had also performed the Living Mermaid.) At the start of July 1891, Samuel appeared as Professor Burnette for two weeks at Shakespeare Shenton's Victoria Hall, Cheltenham, before moving on to Gloucester. Shenton was well known within the variety entertainment world and was a useful contact for Samuel, although perhaps not the most honest character. However, neither did Samuel prove to be.

Frederick Shakespeare Shenton was born in Cheltenham in 1853 to Thomas and Phoebe. He was a printer, bill poster, tobacconist, ticket agent, advertising agent and contractor. He was also a singer, actor, hotel owner and theatre manager of The Assembly Rooms in Cheltenham. In 1891, he became the sole proprietor and manager of the Victoria Music Hall. A review of its opening described the hall as small but comfortable and admirably adapted for purpose. It was to be conducted on strictly respectable lines, and only the best of talent would be on show. The opening week's performers included Miss Kitty Cosgrave, an excellent burlesque dancer and singer. It is fair to say that Shakespeare Shenton was quite a colourful character with a big personality. Over his career, he became familiar with the inside of the law courts, appearing numerous times on a variety of charges. These included selling poor-quality waxwork models, a dispute with a rival bill poster in his hometown and refusing to settle the bill for a "piano van" he had ordered. On another occasion, he was arrested for causing an obstruction by standing in the middle of a pavement and causing twenty pedestrians to step onto the road.

(Living Mermaid Illusion, author's collection.)

CHAPTER EIGHT

THE CHURCHYARD MONSTER

In the summer of 1891, Samuel (now calling himself Mr Burnette) was appearing at the Barton Rooms in Gloucester. He was performing and running a variety show, including his new illusion, The Living Mermaid. While he was there, Samuel met up with his old friend, Frank Lind. At this point, Frank was the manager of the Gloucester Royal Albert Hall and still performing as Dr Lind, an illusionist, mesmerist and conjurer. The Royal Albert Hall was originally the old Boothall and it had been used regularly for entertainment. In 1876, it became a circus venue before transforming into a skating rink and eventually a variety theatre. Local history has it that William Shakespeare probably performed there, and there is now a blue plaque marking the place.

It was in Gloucester that Samuel pulled off the biggest confidence trick of his career. But unfortunately, things weren't going well for Samuel. His show was a disaster, unpopular with audiences, and the weekly takings were so bad that Samuel didn't have enough money to pay for his lodgings. On the Sunday evening, Samuel met up with Frank Lind in a local tavern. Samuel was desperate to come up with a plan to raise enough money to pay his debts and move on to a new venue. Frank was reading the local newspaper, and Samuel spotted the headline, *"WHAT WILL BECOME OF OUR DEAD?"*

The article gave a detailed description of the shocking state of Treadway Cemetery and begged the readers to demand that the Burial Board take action to catch and kill the animal that was boring its way through the coffins, raising the dead and feasting on the bloated bodies of dearly beloved friends and family. The authorities were apparently afraid of the carnivorous reptile and were reluctant to confront it. A suggestion was made that the military be brought in to hunt down the beast and kill it. The newspaper claimed it was the duty of every local citizen to help in the matter and to spare no expense to prevent more disgraceful and disgusting scenes from recurring.

The headline is what set things in motion. Samuel decided that he could turn this situation to his advantage and make some money. Samuel left the tavern in a hurry, returning to his lodgings, where he asked the landlady for the name and address of anyone in the town who sold animals. The very next morning, Samuel set off to see the man she had recommended. The man showed Samuel a variety of animals, including a Peruvian guinea pig, costing ten shillings. Ever the charmer, Samuel convinced his landlady to lend him the money to buy the exotic pet. On Monday morning, Samuel sought out Mr Roberts, proprietor of the Barton Rooms in Gloucester. Through skilful persuasion, Samuel convinced Mr Roberts to lease the hall to him for the week, promising to pay the rent on Saturday. Samuel then delivered an enormous roll of paper and a tin of black paint to Frank Lind, instructing him to create a show bill large enough to hang across the entire front of the Rooms. The finished banner read:

> *CAUGHT AT LAST,*
> *AFTER A SEVERE STRUGGLE!*
> *THE CHURCHYARD MONSTER*
> *WILL BE EXHIBITED HERE FOR THREE DAYS ONLY FROM THURSDAY NEXT.*
> *ADMITTANCE 6d.*

Having spent the last of his money, Samuel borrowed some more from Frank and went to the local newspaper's office, where he had the wording of the poster placed as an advertisement. The editor, who had run the original story, became very excited on hearing that the beast had been caught and insisted that his reporters be allowed to see the animal. Samuel assured him that the reporters could view the animal if they were at the Barton Rooms at eight o'clock that evening.

He then rushed back to Frank and told him that the poster must be hung up outside the hall as soon as possible because reporters were arriving at eight o'clock to see the creature. Frank, still with no clue as to what was happening, by now was in a state of confusion. Samuel cheerfully explained that he was just about to go and catch the "Graveyard Monster" and it was imperative that Frank be at the hall for seven o'clock so that he could see the animal for himself. In the meantime, Samuel went off to finalise and put in place the finer details of his scheme, and timing was everything if the plan was to be a success.

He set off to the local knacker's yard, where he bought a quantity of very ripe horse meat before going to the grocer's, where he obtained a lead-lined tea chest. He cut away the side and fixed some iron rods, then nailed down the lid. Before long, the tea chest looked like a miniature lion's cage. He then filled the box with plenty of straw.

With the cage ready and the guinea pig hidden under his coat, Samuel then headed off to the cemetery, where he prowled around the graveyard shrubbery, creating much noise as he beat the branches with a large stick. All this was observed by an audience of local gravediggers who seemed bemused by his actions.

Suddenly, Samuel shouted, "Help! Help! Here it is! Help!" The gravediggers ran to see what the commotion was, and to their amazement, there was Samuel scrambling between the headstones, waving his stick in the air, chasing after a shiny, black animal. The gravediggers joined in with the chase, running behind Samuel, who was a few yards ahead of them. The hunt went on for some time until Samuel stopped, took aim, threw his stick and struck the animal. Stunned, the animal turned to face the men just as Samuel hurled himself forward, landing on top of the animal. Samuel grabbed the animal and yelled, "It's biting me! It's going to kill me!" He tried to free himself, but for some reason, the beast would not let go and clung on to him. Finally, after much struggling, the exhausted creature became quiet and still.

The gravediggers wanted to take the animal straightaway to the Burial Board and claim the reward that had been offered. But Samuel refused to do any such thing, and after some haggling, he promised a reward of his own, which would be given on Saturday to the man who had helped most in the capture of the beast.

And so, clutching the animal in a firm grip, Samuel raced through the streets, hotly pursued by the Gravediggers. Small children and a few stray dogs joined in with the chase, sensing some excitement not to be missed. Finally, Samuel raced back down to the Barton Rooms, where Frank was waiting. Samuel flew through the door, and Frank instantly closed it, barring entrance to the now considerable crowd which had chased Samuel.

As Frank looked on in sheer astonishment, Samuel placed the animal in the straw in the furthest corner of the cage and threw in some of the putrid meat at the back before putting the cage on top of a tall packing case in the middle of the hall. Just then, a loud banging and knocking at the door announced the arrival of the two reporters from the local newspaper. Samuel and Frank let the reporters in and led them over to the cage, where they were allowed to look over the packing case at the creature. Because the cage contained so much straw, the reporters couldn't even get a glimpse of the animal and had to be content with a description of it from Samuel. After just a few minutes, Samuel ushered the reporters out of the hall.
The next day, the local newspaper headlined the story of the heroic capture of the creature by Mr Burnette. The report included a detailed description of the Churchyard Monster:

"It had eyes like an owl, with feathers upon the front of its head, and hair and a tail resembling that of a rat while its feet looked, for all the world like that of a stoat or weasel."

The Burial Board members were allowed private access to view the animal, and over the next few days, excitement gripped the townsfolk who were eager to see the monster for themselves. Since its capture, pictures of the monster had been selling like hotcakes and became the talk of the town. At eleven o'clock on Thursday morning, the Barton Room doors were opened to the public. The hall was packed, with many people unable to get close enough to the cage to see the animal. As people left the hall, they gave exaggerated descriptions of the creature to those still waiting outside. This intensified the interest and determination of the local people to happily part with their money in order to see the beast for themselves. From eleven o'clock in the morning until ten o'clock at night, people and money poured into the hall.

By Saturday, excitement was at fever pitch, and a continuous stream of people arrived throughout the whole day, and Samuel made a small fortune. However, by Saturday evening, it looked as if his luck and fortune were about to change. Word had begun to spread around the town that the whole affair was nothing more than a hoax to swindle people out of their cash. The gossip grew until a hoard of people gathered outside the hall, demanding to speak to Mr Burnette. Samuel, ever the skilled showman and orator, climbed onto a box and addressed the crowd.

"I have the greatest respect for this honoured town. Do you think that I, a respectable showman, would dare come here and try to defraud its people? No. A thousand times, no! This is a genuine show, and if anyone can prove otherwise, then he can blooming well eat the Churchyard Monster!"
The crowd cheered their appreciation at his remarks until a voice called out from the back, "You are a liar. You bought the animal from me on Monday!" The crowd recognised the gentleman as a local and began to turn on Samuel, demanding justice and their money back. Just at that moment, a young gravedigger, who was also known to locals, shouted out, "That's a lie. I helped the man catch it, and I swear it is the genuine thing!"

With some more persuasive words, Samuel convinced the crowd that his accuser was, in fact, a drunkard who had been refused entry to the hall and was out for revenge. The crowd then turned on the man who had accused Samuel and jostled him away while at the same time hailing Samuel as a hero. Samuel, who was still on top of the box in the thick of the crowd, questioned the young gravedigger as to the true events of the animal's capture. Then, in front of the crowd, the gravedigger explained what had taken place in the graveyard and how Mr Burnette had fearlessly caught the monster. The crowd was won over, and for two more hours, people gladly paid to view the Churchyard Monster.

At some point during the three days, Samuel, ever the businessman, had entered into negotiations with Mr Shakespeare Shenton, the proprietor of the Theatre Royal Cheltenham, offering to sell him the animal. A sum of three guineas was agreed upon, and Samuel promised to hand over the animal on Saturday evening after the show. When the doors finally closed, the iron cage containing the creature was handed over to its new owner, and Samuel congratulated himself on his earnings.
On the following Monday morning, the local newspaper carried the headline:

BARNUM OUTDONE! The report explained how the townsfolk had indeed been the victims of an enormous hoax carried out by Mr Burnette. The gentleman in the crowd who had accused Burnette was the owner of a little pet animal which his children loved to play with. Burnette had seen the animal and offered to buy it, saying he was a conjurer and wanted it for his act. The gentleman was reluctant to sell it on account of how fond his children were of the little pet. Eventually, the sum of ten shillings was agreed upon, with the understanding that the gentleman could have the little pet back any time he wanted. According to the gentleman, Burnette then put the animal in his pocket and ran off to the cemetery. Once there, Burnette staged the whole affair of the capture, making sure he had witnesses to vouch for the unfolding events. When the reporters arrived at the hall to view the creature, they could only make out a bundle of straw inside the box and complained.

Mr Burnette explained that he could not guarantee that the creature would not attack them. Instead, he gave a vivid description of the creature, which was then reproduced by a local artist and sold as a genuine likeness. Putrid, rotten meat had been bought from a local butcher and spread around the inside of the cage to add effect to the spectacle when, in fact, the little animal was fed milk and bread. The young, naive gravedigger had given an honest account of what he saw, and when he stood up for Burnette in the face of an angry crowd, he probably saved him from a lynching.

And so Samuel was able to settle his debts and still have a considerable profit in his pockets.
And as for Mr Shenton, the new owner of the creature, whenever anyone asked about the little animal curled up on the rug in front of the fire, he would say, "Why, that's a dear little Peruvian guinea pig!"
As a postscript to this chapter of Samuel's career, on 3 August 1891, The Citizen newspaper printed the following report:

> *"The Churchyard Monster."*
> *– A good deal of speculation has been rife as to the nature of this beast, which has been on show at the Gloucester Assembly Rooms, and we hear that the minds of nervous and hysterical women have been disturbed by its description. Mr Daniel Roberts, who has a knowledge of natural history, has pronounced the "monster" (and we understand that the accuracy of his judgement has not been impugned) to be nothing more terrible than a Peruvian Guinea Pig.*

It is a testament to Samuel's audacity and boldness as a showman because a week after his grand hoax, he and Frank Lind were back on stage in Gloucester, appearing alongside Gus Levaine, an established theatre owner and entertainer.

> *Royal Albert Theatre Gloucester.*
> *Grand Special Performance in aid of the Gloucester Infirmary and Children's Hospital. Tonight, and for this night only, Professor Burnette will introduce "She" At The Stake. Dr Lind and Gus Levaine will also appear. Tickets can be obtained from Mr Lind, Manager.*
> (Gloucester Citizen 11 August 1891)

Gus Levaine, whose real name was Harry Augustus Lawes, was born in 1854 in Shoreditch. He started off as an engineer's assistant before entering the world of music halls and theatre. In 1875, he married Elizabeth Margaret Tabrar (Lizzie Tabra/ Lizzie Tabrar), and one year later, they appeared as a musical double act on stage in Walworth, south London. This developed into a musical comedy act, including burlesque sketches. But neither their stage act nor their marriage was to last. After less than ten years and four children together, Lizzie left Gus. In 1887, she tried twice to bring a charge of desertion against him. However, once in court, she admitted that she had voluntarily left her husband and refused to return to the marital home. The case was dismissed. Lizzie died in 1896 in tragic circumstances. A verdict of accidental death was declared after she apparently fell over a bannister and landed at the bottom of a flight of stairs, sustaining a head injury.

Gus Levaine became a big name within the theatre community. He toured with his successful act, The Levaine Trio, with great success before creating his theatre company, The Levaine Troupe, which toured Scotland and England. A year after Lizzie walked out on their marriage, Gus became manager of The Grand Variety Hall in Northampton. This was the first of several appointments as theatre manager that he held. He later became manager of the Alhambra Nottingham, Marina Theatre Ramsgate, Coventry Hippodrome, Shadfriars Hall Boston, The Matlock Pavilion, Raikes Hall Blackpool and The Empire Theatre of Varieties in Coventry. In addition, he managed, directed, produced and starred in concert parties and pantomimes all over the country, both north and south of the Border. Gus Levaine married twice more. In 1891, he married Emma Elaine Wilkinson, and they had a daughter. In 1918, he married Fannie Collins, a stage performer and they had nine children together. Gus Levaine died in 1936 in Derbyshire, aged 81.

Years later, in 1929, Samuel gave an account of the hoax in an article entitled *Leaves From a Showman's Life,* which appeared in The Thistle Christmas Special. In the article, Samuel elaborates a little more about the adventure:

My assistant was at the door who travelled with me. I said to him, "Now Dick we shall have to work up a sensation, it is getting quiet, you will have to be bitten by this monster." He said, "No thanks Governor." "Well," I said, "the next thing is to make it appear that you have been bitten." So, with the use of a little dragon's blood, some linen and a sling, he looked the part. He told me that for the three nights, he got over £4 from sympathising patrons who felt sorry for him. I might tell you I had never handled so much money for myself in a very long time and this was the commencement of my success.

I wonder where in Gloucester Samuel was able to buy some dragon's blood and how much it cost? One thing is for certain, he was a wonderful storyteller. The 1901 article on the Graveyard Monster, which appeared in *The Showman* newspaper, was a humorous three-page spread. The report stated that the hoax had been concocted by Mr Burnette and Mr Lind together, both reaping the monetary rewards at the expense of the townsfolk. This article was strongly refuted by Frank Lind when he wrote a letter to the Editor of The Showman to put the record straight:

Dear Sir,
My attention has been drawn to your article in issue of 4 April, entitled "Barnum Outdone." The writer of such article has mis – spelt my name, which is spelt "Lind" and not "Lynn." He says he can vouch for the truth of what he states, but I must say, he has grossly exaggerated in many cases and in others mis – represented things, and in fairness to myself as well as to Mr Burnette, an old friend of mine, I think you should insert this letter. In the first place, I was not running a variety company in the sense your writer states, and I was, at that period, manager and part proprietor of the Royal Albert Theatre, Gloucester; and as regards my doing bad business, and not being able to find funds for the treasury, it is grossly false, as at that time I was doing good business. Mr Burnette, at that time was not in any way connected with me, but we, being old friends, he came to see me when he came to Gloucester, and in conversation I mentioned that as business was quiet with him (at that time he was showing The Mermaid and other Illusions) it would be a grand thing if he could manage to get hold of this particular animal that was causing a sensation. As to where he got it, or how he got it, was no business of mine. The animal in question, when I saw it, I pronounced to be a giant specimen of a foreign guinea pig; not being a naturalist I could not say the species, but this I will state, that it was not so harmless as your informant states. Naturalists who saw it, pronounced it to be a giant specimen of Peruvian Guinea Pig, with exceedingly long claws or talons. Needless to say, that it did pull up the fortunes of my friend Burnette; but beyond doing what I could for him for "Auld Lang Syne" I had no further connection with the matter, and there are many others who know the same. Therefore, this should be inserted in fairness to me; those who know me, know that I would not give my name or countenance to what your informant calls a bare–faced swindle. I like the truth always, but don't like to read my name mentioned in the way your informant puts it, more especially as he so misrepresents and distorts facts.
I beg to remain, Mr Editor, Yours faithfully H. Frank Lind, F.O.S. Illusionist and Entertainer, and Exhibition Proprietor. Lind's Waxworks Leeds, 14 April 1901.
(The Showman 19 April 1901)

It is evident from his letter that Frank was the one who inadvertently or otherwise gave Samuel the idea, which grew and grew, eventually becoming one enormous hoax. Obviously, Frank Lind wanted to disassociate himself from this act of fraud to preserve his fragile reputation. But it was extremely hypocritical of Frank to claim he liked the truth, for he was not an honest man by any stretch of the imagination! His reference to "Auld Lang Syne", I think, implies that he is admitting to helping his friend, Mr Burnette, to some extent but is adamant that he had no part in the actual fraud. Samuel's account states that Frank helped finance the swindle and even made the exhibition banner. Samuel happily admitted to the fraud and laughed it off as a colourful adventure. However, we shall never know Frank Lind's exact involvement or extent.

CHAPTER NINE

NORTH, SOUTH, EAST AND WEST

After his exploits in Gloucester, Samuel continued to perform all over the country for the remainder of 1891, presenting his shows, The Living Mermaid and She At The Stake, including a return visit to The Royal Aquarium. In October of that year, he was in Exeter with a new business venture:

Wanted. Living Novelties with Paintings. Freaks preferred. Share or Salary. Fred Burnette, Shop Exhibition, 35 Shore Street, Exeter.
(The Era 10 October 1891)

In 1892, another daughter, Daisy May, was born. She was baptised in the church of The Holy Trinity in Bath. Samuel is listed as a conjuror on the baptism record, but Daisy May's father was clearly much more than that, as this review from the Bridport News testifies.

Rousden Village School 1892:
This year, Professor Burnette the celebrated wizard from Bath, was engaged for a third time and though an old friend to the Rousden people, the Professor managed to introduce much that was novel in leger de main and comic character. His "Ally Sloper" get up was quite perfect and caused roars of laughter. The banjo and negro pieces also afforded a deal of enjoyment and there was a full audience on both evenings.
(Bridport News 1 January 1892)

Samuel was very clever to include his Ally Sloper act because it was a huge favourite amongst audiences. Alley Sloper was a comic strip character who is often attributed to the novelist Charles Henry Ross, although, in fact, it was his wife Marie Duval's creation. The character appeared in comic strip format around 1867 in the *Judy* (similar to *Punch*) magazine. Alley Sloper was a red-nosed, lazy schemer, a drunkard and a con man, sloping through alleyways to avoid his landlord and other creditors. Although he was a fictional character, he became a hero amongst Victorian readers and was such a phenomenon that he developed a life outside the magazine. Music hall comedians and entertainers took on the character and developed their own Alley Sloper acts. Alley Sloper became a slang term of the time, referring to a poverty-stricken tenant who sloped off to avoid paying the rent collector. However, for all his bad points, the character appealed to a wide readership because he was ever the optimist, a working-class patriot and a royalist. By 1896, one newspaper argued that Alley Sloper was the most famous fictional character there had ever been. There is an argument that Alley Sloper inspired the screen character of W. C Fields.

On 2 April 1892, Samuel was in high demand. An advert was placed in The Era by Mr Baker, an agent in London looking for Fred Burnette to contact him because of an opening for an exhibition shop in London. On the same day, in the same newspaper, Madame D'Arc placed an advert:

Wanted. Fred Burnette of "She" illusion to communicate with Madame D'Arc relative to Easter engagement. Victoria Rooms Cardiff.

Although not apparent at the time, it was this small but not insignificant advert that was to have an enormous impact on Samuel's future. It was to bring him to Wales and connect with the D'Arcs, an experience which would change his life forever in more ways than one. The same week that Madame D'Arc placed the advert, Samuel appeared on the same bill as Marie Lloyd at the Grand Theatre in Liverpool, where he came in for "a fair share of the applause".

This must have been a highlight in his stage career because this was a significant bill on which to appear, as Marie Lloyd was already a famous music hall performer who headlined many London West End shows.

Marie had made her debut at the Grecian Halls when she was only 15 years old, which set her on the road to stardom. Not a conventional beauty, she held audiences captive with her knowing smile and cheeky wink, not to mention her trademark high kicks showing a glimpse of petticoats and bloomers. She was in such demand and so popular with audiences that music composers wrote songs specifically for her.

Samuel secured the engagement for an Easter performance with Madame D'Arc in Cardiff, where he presented his new act, "Una". After his Easter engagement in Cardiff, he secured a month appearing at Shakespeare Shenton's Victoria Hall in Cheltenham. Samuel then placed notices in the press advertising four new illusions and freaks as part of his act, looking for work in shops, piers and gardens. After a brief appearance at the Alhambra, performing a musical entertainment, Samuel returned to Fell's in Glasgow.

Wanted. Known. Professor Fred Burnette. F.O.S Greater success than ever. Finished seven weeks comfortable engagement at Fell's Varieties Glasgow. Address Kingsmead Street, Bath. (The Era 1 October 1892)

Straight after his performance with Fell's, Samuel was on stage in Motherwell:

Saturday Night Concert. Artistes for tonight.
The McConnell Family Joe Edmonds Negro Comedian
Fred Burnette Comic Vocalist
Comedians, Vocalists, Instrumentalists, Burlesque Actors &c.
(Motherwell Times 22 October 1892)

The first half of 1893 was a difficult time for Samuel, and he was accepting work wherever he could find it. Although he appeared on bills with the likes of Marie Lloyd, his big break in show business was proving to be as elusive as ever, and yet, he wasn't prepared to give up and settle back home in Bath with Jessie Rose and their children. Being so ambitious and driven, believing in his own worth and ability, meant that he was back on the road, travelling from one job to another. It must have been soul-destroying at times because he struggled to find his big break in theatre. Once again, he was often performing to small, provincial audiences in school rooms and local halls. He wasn't always able to secure work for his conjuring act and had to take whatever he was offered. As an accomplished musician, he was able instead to accept several small turns where he played the banjo, fiddle, cello and even musical water glasses.

The parish tea was held in the Infant Schoolroom at Batheaston, where 140 sat down to a tea provided by Mr Lavington. After the tables were cleared, a conjuring entertainment was given by Professor Burnette.
(Bath Chronicle and Weekly Gazette 5 January 1893)

At Evercreech an entertainment consisting of sleight of hand tricks was given in the schoolroom by Professor and Madame Burnette. The various tricks were very cleverly executed. There was a large attendance and the proceeds were given to the village lighting fund.
(Western Chronicle 17 February 1893)

By June 1893, he had made his way over the border back to Wales. It is possible that Samuel saw the following advert in The Era, and it was enough to appeal to his ambitious character:

Wanted to Let, in Principal Street Aberdare population 40000, Six Roomed Shop, suitable for Waxworks, Bazars, Auctions, Tank Shows, any Novelty. A fortune to be made by enterprising man. One room 30 ft by 14th on ground floor. Apply Evans Caterer, Aberdare.
(The Era 3 June 1893)

No doubt it was the phrase "a fortune to be made by enterprising man" that appealed to Samuel and prompted him to make the journey to Aberdare in Wales to seek his fortune:

Wanted to let in Principal Street, Aberdare, large shop suitable for illusions, waxworks, bazaars, auctions. Huge success of Professor Burnette. Vacant after 29 July. Evans Caterer Aberdare.
(The Era 29 July 1893)

However, it is unlikely that Samuel made his fortune in Aberdare because a fortnight after finishing there, he travelled to Cardiff, where he appeared again for the D'Arc family:

D'Arc's Grand Waxworks And Hall Of Varieties, Victoria Rooms, St Mary's Street, Cardiff, Special Engagement, One Week Only, of Professor Burnette's Living Marvels and Stage Performances. The champion show of Wales. Open all day. Admission 3d children 2d.
(Western Gazette 8 August 1893)

Much has been written about the D'Arcs, a world-renowned family of waxwork modellers, marionette makers and entertainers. Lambert D'Arc had learned his craft while working for Tussauds before setting up his own business, which became a family affair involving his wife and all of his children. D'Arcs marionettes had travelled much of the world and had established a superior reputation for first-class entertainment. D'Arc's had been established in Cardiff since 1884, and by the time Samuel performed there in 1893, their popularity had not diminished.

This appearance revealed to Samuel what a successful business the family had built up. The Cardiff waxworks had the most up-to-date models, comprising the celebrities of the time. The marionettes displayed mechanical perfection with moving limbs, eyes and mouths. Even the hand-painted scenery and backdrops were moving mechanical images. Samuel would have walked through each room where the different tableaux were exhibited with background instrumental music for added atmosphere. He must have been enthralled and amazed at the clever pantomimes and stories told by the marionettes and their puppet masters. Victorian audiences throughout the country had a fascination for magic, freak shows, and waxworks. But this was an eye-opener for Samuel because D'Arc's was a polished, quality entertainment experience. Moreover, he saw that a waxworks exhibition could be so much more than simply displaying static figures. From his experience at D'Arc's, a seed of an idea was planted, a seed that would take root and germinate over time in Samuel's ambitious imagination.

Samuel's reconnection with the D'Arc family resulted in life-changing decisions and choices in his professional and personal life. It is more than likely that Samuel kept in constant contact with the D'Arc family, possibly revisiting them in Cardiff in a business capacity, learning the tricks of their trade. Samuel spent some considerable time trying to establish his reputation in Wales and make a success of his new business projects because it was around this time that he began to diversify into the D'Arc's world of marionettes, freak shows and waxworks. By late 1894, Samuel was still in Wales, but it was an apparent struggle as he felt the need to convince audiences that all was well:

Wanted, Old Friends To Know, Fred Burnette doing good business. Big show in preparation. Now at 55 Commercial Street, Newport Monmouthshire.
(The Era 8 December 1894)

It is unclear how long the show at Newport lasted, but by the middle of the following year, 1895, Samuel was in Bristol attempting to put together a new show:

> *Wanted. Novelties (with paintings) for best position, Castle Street. Share or certainty. Fred Burnette*
> *23 Castle Street, Bristol.*
> (The Era 3 August 1895)

After several years on the road, whether through bad luck, bad timing or lack of experience, the venture was a financial disaster, leaving Samuel with an empty bank account. Throughout these years, Samuel's wife, Jessie Rose, was still living in Bath. In 1894, Jessie Rose had given birth to a second son, Herbert Alford, just months before Samuel's show opened in Newport. On Herbert's christening record, Samuel is an Actor. Life for Jessie Rose could not have been easy, trying to make ends meet with five small children to look after. Even with the support of family who lived nearby, with Samuel absent for much of the time, Jessie Rose must have struggled on a daily basis. Basic necessities like food, rent, coal and clothes had to be paid for. As a travelling entertainer, Samuel would have had his own expenses to cover, including lodgings, transport and rent for venues. In addition, there would have been the added cost of stage clothes and props for his conjuring tricks, not forgetting a cut of the profits going to Madame Hilda.

By this time, Samuel's father was no longer working as a blacksmith. At the age of 54, he was an invalid living at home and was being looked after by his wife. Samuel's youngest brother was still at school, but all of his other siblings were employed, bringing money into the household. Even his twelve-year-old brother was a part-time errand boy. Samuel could have chosen to give up the notion of show business and settle down as a family man with a regular paying job as his brothers and sisters had done, but that was never part of his plan. In a 1901 interview in The Showman, Samuel mentions his failed business during the early years and how this prompted him to accept the position as Chairman Manager of The Pavilion Music Hall in Bath. The interview article gives no dates nor details of how long Samuel held that position. It could have been a matter of months or possibly years.

Throughout 1895, Samuel expanded his business by operating exhibition shops in Bath, Bristol, and Exeter. It was around this time that he dropped his Professor Burnette, as there was no mention of the Professor in any of the trade newspapers after this time. By 1896, he had travelled back across the border into Wales with a much bigger show, where he ran into a spot of bother with the authorities:

> *NEITHER A FAT MAN NOR A THIN WOMAN*
> *The Newport Police told the magistrates at the Ukside Borough Police Court on Monday that Mr Fred Burnette was the proprietor of a show which was being exhibited at 55 Commercial Street, and that owing to the members of the company appearing in character dress in the doorway people stopped outside the shop and the footway was frequently blocked. The Magistrate's Clerk inquired the nature of the show, and asked if it was a fat man or thin woman that was being exhibited. Inspector Brooks replied that it was the "Miser's Ghost." Mr Burnette now expressed his desire to keep within the requirements of the law, and said that he had put a man on in private clothes to keep the pavement clear. The Magistrates, however, imposed a fine of 20 shillings.*
> (South Wales Daily News 15 September 1896.)

CHAPTER TEN

MR TUSSAUD, MR STIFF AND THE WAXWORKS

Samuel disappeared from public view in 1895 and wouldn't surface again until 1897 in Southampton. He had a year-long engagement there with his new Electroscope exhibition show. At the start of 1898, he placed a wanted ad in The Stage, looking for smart, respectable, sober people for short, dramatic sketches for his new show, which he promised was opening shortly in London. The advert warned that the pay was low but guaranteed. There is no evidence to prove that the London show went ahead, but if it did, it couldn't have lasted that long because, in January 1899, Samuel was in Burnley, Lancashire, with his "Ghost Show." Later that same year, he was running his Electric Wonder Exhibition in Worcester.

Samuel was back on the road, performing and entertaining audiences once again. But it was around this time that he stopped appearing as Professor Burnette and began to fully embrace the role of Frederick Rendell Burnette. There is one more short mention of Samuel in the provinces before his career took a new path. In 1900, he appeared at the Lyric Theatre of Varieties in Bath:

> *Mr Rendell Burnette is again appearing with the concertophone which is much appreciated.*
> (The Era 28 April 1900)

The concertophone appears to have been a type of phonograph, a machine that had the ability to record and replay sounds etched onto a cylinder. It is possible that Samuel used the machine to simply play pre-recorded music to the audience. However, it is equally possible that Samuel used it as a tool in his act by recording himself, perhaps even with some audience participation.

Shortly after Samuel's appearance playing the concertophone in Bath, he decided to move Jessie Rose and the children to London. It may be that the last few years spent on the road with his conjuring shows had proved too difficult for Samuel. He must have come to the painful realisation that he was not going to achieve fame or fortune as a magician. However, after years in the entertainment industry, Samuel was aware of what audiences wanted, so he decided to embark upon a brand-new career for himself. How he was able to finance the move and set up in London is anyone's guess, but he had proved in the past that he could talk a good talk, and over the years, he had made sound connections within the show business world. One of those London connections was a man by the name of Mr Stiff, more of whom we shall hear about later. However, I do think that Samuel's reputation for being a reliable, hard worker would have stood him in good stead.

The move to London wasn't the only significant decision that Samuel made. He saw this as a new start and an opportunity to reinvent himself. From this point onwards, Samuel was only ever known as Frederick Rendell Burnette. However, he made "Frederick Rendell Burnette" not only a business name but a change of persona. As Frederick, he was an ambitious businessman and successful entrepreneur who was unafraid to take risks.

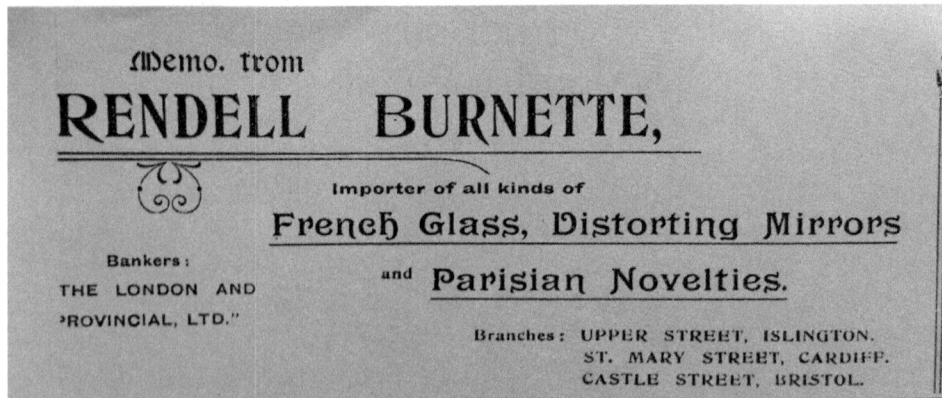

(Business card, image credit: Ian Armstrong.)

By January 1901, Samuel had opened at least two waxwork exhibition shops in London. Rendell Burnette's Grand Promenade of Mechanical and Electric Wonders was in Mare Street, Hackney. A gas engine and electric motor ensured that the models were in constant motion. There were the usual waxwork displays, with everything from Queen Victoria playing the piano to marching soldiers at Southampton Docks. But this was a substantial shop as it contained a couple of peep shows, an exhibition room for displaying the latest human "freaks", and a shooting gallery.

> *Altogether this is probably one of the most interesting shows in London, and whenever I feel a trifle despondent, I shall certainly go to Mare Street, and rely on Mr. Burnette to cheer me up.*
(The Showman 15 March 1901)

Samuel's second shop was at 104 Upper Street, Islington, with the family living on the premises. This address had been the location of a waxwork's exhibition hall since 1888, which included "Grande tableaux" and instruments of torture. Jessie Rose helped to run the business, and their daughter, Jessie Emily, cleaned and repaired the models.

(Postcard of Upper Street from author's collection.)

This exhibition was very popular with Londoners because Samuel had incorporated his mechanical and electric models into the display, including a Chamber of Horrors. At the same time, he had started another business of imported French glass, distorting mirrors and Parisian novelties, which were used to good effect in his shops.

At the entrance to 104 Upper Street, you were met by a life-size model of Dick Turpin and his horse, Black Bess. On entering the premises, you would encounter a warren of staircases leading to sumptuous tableaux on every level, including Baden Powell defending Mafeking, the Magi at Bethlehem and returning servicemen from the Boer War. At the top of the building was The Throne Room, consisting of seventeen figures, all dressed in court attire. Of course, the throne in the centre of the display was empty following the death of Queen Victoria. No waxwork shop would be complete without a Chamber of Horrors, and this one was not for the faint-hearted. The tableaux displayed scenes of murder and suicide in all their gory detail, with life-like models caught in the most heinous acts and forever frozen in time. The Showman magazine declared that, "Nowhere could you have had more beauty, more real art, or more blood for your penny than at Burnette's."

Samuel had chosen his location well. Islington was fast becoming a waxwork hot spot. There were already several established waxwork shops on Upper Street, including two owned by Frederick Stewart and another run by Walter Stiff. Waxwork Exhibition shops were more than simply displays of waxwork models. Proprietors used novelties, freaks, tableaux vivants, variety acts and touring performers to entice the paying public across the door in an attempt to educate, entertain and often shock audiences. In some of the larger halls, cinematograph shows had become part of the entertainment. Through the influence of Mr Lionel Bartram, Samuel gradually got together a collection of mechanical models, and since starting in this line, he became the proprietor of three London shop shows.

Not content to stay in London and reap the rewards of his latest new venture, the call of the road was too strong for Samuel to ignore. Once he had acquired enough models, marionettes and staging, Samuel took his exhibition on tour around the country, leaving Jessie Rose at Upper Street to run the London side of the business. In January 1901, while Samuel was away, Jessie Rose had to deal with an incident of assault at the waxworks.

John Doherty had been refused entry to the waxworks because of his boisterous behaviour. Unfortunately, he forced his way in and proceeded to damage several waxwork models, including a figure of Amelia Dyer and a prison chaplain. Doherty was removed from the premises by a police constable and later appeared at Clerkenwell Court on a charge of wilful damage. Mr Doherty expressed his regret and stated his intention to pay the full amount of £3 to Mrs Burnette, manageress, as compensation for the damage he had caused. The Evening News carried a brief but inaccurate account of the episode, stating that 104 Upper Street was the property of Mr. Stiff. As a result of this inaccuracy, Walter Stiff's lawyer wrote to the editor to explain that his client had no connection, interest, or business with 104 Upper Street. He firmly pointed out that his client was the only wax modeller in the world bearing the name 'Stiff' and was at a loss as to how his name had become linked to this establishment. The lawyer demanded that the editor print the letter in the next issue and give it full publicity.

Walter Stiff and Samuel were close competitors. Stiff's waxwork shop located only four doors down from Samuel's. Stiff wanted no association with F.R Burnette's waxworks as a result of a previous business deal that went sour. While this would have been an unpleasant experience for Jessie Rose, for me, a more unpleasant aspect is the fact that the waxwork exhibition had a model of Amelia Dyer, a serial child killer who had been a baby farmer for a period of 30 years. Victorian audiences loved to be shocked and certainly had a taste for things macabre, but this is simply distasteful by today's standards. I can't help but feel some sympathy for Mr Doherty.

(Samuel, image credit: Ian Armstrong.)

The Upper Street waxworks were so successful with London audiences that in 1901, Samuel was interviewed for an article in *The Showman*. *The* reporter describes Frederick as "*One of England's best-known shop show proprietors, who was a genial and good-hearted individual.* The interview took place in the Burnette "comfortably furnished" parlour. Samuel demonstrated to the reporter how all the tables, chairs and other pieces in the parlour had been constructed to conveniently collapse and fold into travelling cases. Samuel had packing down to a fine art to include every other household item that might be required during his travels. *"Mr Burnette can leave one neighbourhood in the morning and be comfortably established in a totally different quarter the same evening."*

The description of the parlour furniture suggests that when Samuel was off touring with his show, Jessie Rose was left sitting in an empty parlour because Samuel had taken the home comforts with him. It appears that he spent a great deal of time away from home with his travelling exhibition, leaving the family behind in Upper Street yet ensuring that he had all the comforts of home at his disposal. In 1902, Samuel was still running his waxwork business from 104 Upper Street with Jessie Rose in charge while he was away from home. While this business venture flourished, however, it wasn't long before disaster struck.

> *A waxwork exhibition was the scene of a serious fire last night. While some gas fitters were at work on the premises, owned by Mr F Burnette, the showroom on the ground floor suddenly burst into flames. The local firemen were unable to prevent the entire premises being very seriously damaged.*
> (The Globe 28 May 1902)

There is no further information to say how severe the damage to the models and marionettes was, but the business at Upper Street was able to continue. Meanwhile, Samuel continued with his travelling exhibition around the towns and cities of England, which would have provided the family with a steady income. Then, disaster struck again, but fortunately for Samuel, he managed by sheer luck to avoid any financial repercussions.

After a successful exhibition at Crystal Palace, Louis Tussaud, the great, great-grandson of Madame Tussaud, sold off his waxwork models. Walter Stiff bought some of these models and added to them with some of his own. Stiff then opened several exhibitions across London, advertising his shows as branches of Louis Tussaud's waxworks from Regent Street. Samuel purchased some models from Stiff and opened his own exhibition in Islington, using the Tussaud name. Louis Tussaud planned to take action against both men, but his lawyer advised him to take each case individually. Tussaud decided to act against Mr Stiff first.

Tussaud had his day in court with Mr Stiff, but the case was dismissed. No further legal action was brought against Samuel, which was lucky as he could have been looking at financial damage from court costs and, more importantly, damage to his reputation. He must have realised what a lucky escape he had because, after the court incident, there is no evidence that he had any further dealings with Mr Stiff, possibly having got the measure of the man and not wanting his name linked in any respect with him. A wise decision, as Walter Stiff eventually ended up in prison.

In 1904, Mr stiff pleaded guilty to a charge of having endeavoured to obtain by false pretences from London City Council two sums of money, £7247 and £3903. Stiff's so-called sister-in-law, Emma Mary Flood, aged 35, was charged with wilful and corrupt perjury, and his so-called niece, Emma Flood, aged 30, was charged with conspiracy to obtain money by fraudulent means. During court proceedings, it was proved that the women were not related to Stiff, and some unsavoury details regarding their murky relationship were revealed. Stiff's fraudulent account books, which were presented in court, were his undoing. Stiff was sentenced to eight years of penal servitude with an extra nine months for conspiracy to run concurrently.

CHAPTER ELEVEN

THE AUCTION, THE WORKHOUSE AND AN AFFAIR

At some point in 1902, Samuel and Jessie Rose moved from Upper Street to Fairbridge Road. On 4th January 1903, their new baby son, Sam Edwin Redvers Rendell, was christened in Islington. On the Baptism entry, Samuel was listed as an engineer. Jessie Rose would have been almost forty when she gave birth, and although there would have been much happiness and celebration in the Rendell household, but it wasn't to last. With a brand-new infant, Jessie Rose was left alone in London as Samuel was absent from the family for much of the time with his travelling show. The same month that baby Sam was christened, Samuel was working in Bristol:

> *Madame D'Arc is presenting a series of six splendid wax tableau entitled "The Road to Ruin" at her well-known establishment at 27 Castle Street, Bristol which needless to say is being highly patronised. Higher up the street is Rendell Burnette's Electric Promenade that recently had a successful run in and around London.*
> (The Showman 16th January 1903)

Samuel's time in London was running out, which was a consequence of two significant events, both of which occurred in 1903. In March of that year, the waxworks shop at 104 Upper Street was sold at auction. According to the newspaper report at the time, the auctioneer had been instructed by the owner to sell the entire business because of a family bereavement. The only family bereavement to have occurred around this time was the death of Samuel's father in December of the previous year, leaving an estate worth £155 10s 10d and Samuel as executor.

104 Upper Street was a very substantial and successful business, so the decision to sell could not have been taken lightly. There was more to this than meets the eye. What plans did Samuel have for the money?

The auction was held on Tuesday 24th March at one o'clock which many well-known showmen attended. Samuel had employed the best auctioneer in the business. "The Silver King" was a well-respected member of the fairground community, and his very presence guaranteed a good turnout. More than two hundred lots from the waxwork shop alone were up for sale, and those present included showmen that Samuel may have known from his younger years spent with the minstrel company. According to The Era newspaper, they included Charles Birch, Frederick Stewart, A. E. Pickard, Mr. Baily, Clarence Barron, William Lionel Bartram, David Adams, Alf Balls, Ernest Gambert Baines, Louis Tussaud, and many others. The Throne Room generated the most interest among the bidders, and eventually, it was sold to Mr Barron for £110. Mr Bartram secured Dick Turpin and his horse for thirty guineas, which was considered a bargain. The Silver King had created an atmosphere of tense excitement by deliberately leaving the contents of the Chamber of Horrors as the final lots of the proceedings. Mr Bartram bought the personal belongings of Edgar Edwards, the murderer, for £56 10s, and Pickard bought Mrs Dyson's confession for £42 10s. By six o'clock, the sale of waxworks, scenery and props was concluded. The Silver King then led the audience to his own showground, where he auctioned off a variety of fairground items.

As with many people connected with Samuel, the auctioneer, "The Silver King," was a colourful, larger-than-life character of some renown. There is much conflicting information available about Tom Norman's life, particularly his early years. Like many showmen, Norman was not his real name. Tom Noakes was the son of a butcher, born in 1860 in Sussex and one of at least sixteen children. Some accounts claim that he ran away from home as a young teenager to join a travelling show. He arrived in London, where he worked as a butcher's assistant before going into partnership with a man who owned a Penny Gaff shop in Islington who exhibited Madame Electra.

During the19th century, Penny gaff shops provided cheap entertainment for the poorer classes, which was so called because the entrance fee was a penny, and a gaff was Victorian cockney slang for a place or house of amusement. An evening's entertainment would provide musical turns, comedy acts and short plays. However, London Penny Gaff shows had a more unsavoury nature as the majority of them offered freak shows as the main entertainment. Interestingly, the tale of Sweeny Todd made its debut as early as 1846 in a Penny Gaff.

Norman went on to run several freak show exhibition shops, which were extremely popular with Victorian audiences. As he claims in his autobiography, *"You could indeed exhibit anything in those days. Yes, anything from a needle to an anchor, a flea to an elephant, a bloater you could exhibit as a whale. It was not the show, it was the tale you told."* His career flourished throughout the early 1800s, and eventually, he had thirteen Penny Gaff shops around London. Sometime around 1883/84, he became involved with Joseph Merrick when he took over the London management of the "Elephant Man". Norman's management only lasted for a few months as his shop was closed by the police. In 1896, he married Amy Rayner, and after the birth of his first son, he became an auctioneer for showmen, fairgrounds and theatrical businesses around the country. At the same time, Norman kept his Penny Gaff shops in London and continued to exhibit his travelling freak shows, including his famous travelling midget troupe.

He eventually retired from the fairground business but continued as an auctioneer and became involved with buying and selling horses for circuses and pantomimes. Norman became involved with the Temperance Movement in later years and was vice-president of the Van Dwellers Protection Association. "The Silver King" was considered to be the best auctioneer of his time, so it is no surprise that Samuel engaged his services to ensure the best prices for his Upper Street business. The fact that the auction took five hours or more to complete indicates the size of Samuel's business.

Many of the buyers at the auction were members of the Showmen and Van Dwellers Association and were all known to one another. These were some of the great and good travelling showmen of the time and were well respected within the circus and fairground world:

Mr Birch:
Mr Charles Birch was apparently one of the wealthiest showmen in Scotland and was known as the "Scottish Barnum". He owned numerous freak shows and waxwork establishments all around Scotland and England, stretching from London to Aberdeen and places in between. He had a reputation for being honest, straight-talking and the most genial of men, and as a result, was a well-respected traveller. Birch held more Scottish exhibition licences than any other showman and continually expanded his business empire. In late 1901, he put together a mammoth combination of entertainments for a travelling show in Belfast and Dublin. The show included freaks, musicians, dancers, magicians, illusionists, acrobats and gymnasts. It was such a large-scale show that special train carriages were required to be built for the touring company. Of his many numerous Scottish venues, three were in Aberdeen. In 1902, the authorities tried to close them down on the grounds that they were unsafe to the public and the land was required for the University improvements. However, thanks to a petition raised by the people of Aberdeen, Charles Birch was allowed to continue his business. Because of the heavy-handedness of the authorities, Birch gained much sympathy and support from the local working-class Aberdonians, and his business continued to thrive.

Mr Stewart:
Frederick Stewart (born Frederick Pilfold) married Lily Knight in 1887 when he was only eighteen years old, and together, they had five children. Soon after their marriage, Frederick changed his name and began his career on Brighton Pier with his Flea Circus entertainment. He toured the British Isles with his troupe of performing fleas before giving it up for a career in wax.

Stewart gathered together a collection of models, which he first exhibited in Dundee. It was such a success that he went on tour around Scotland with his waxwork show before settling in Edinburgh, where, in 1895, he opened his permanent "penny show" at 164 - 166 High Street. For an extra penny, visitors could view the more "exciting" attractions. The show was an immediate success and, over the years, continued to grow in popularity with locals and visitors alike.

It wasn't long before Stewart expanded his business to London, opening an exhibition at 108 Upper Street, four doors along from Samuel's waxwork shop, and then a second exhibition at 24 Upper Street. Interestingly, Stewart appointed Harry Addison, of Farini and Barnum fame, as the new Upper Street shop manager. Stewart employed Albert De Witt as his wax figure maker, a man known for his skilled attention to detail in creating realistic models. Walter Stiff had previously employed de Witt before joining Stewart's company. Frederick and Lily's marriage didn't last very long because, in 1905, he divorced Lily and sought custody of the children on the grounds of her adultery. His waxworks in Edinburgh and London were so successful that Frederick opened another business in Aberdeen and at Cowcaddens in Glasgow. He also created a travelling exhibition show that toured all over Scotland.

It was sometime around 1910, while still based in Edinburgh, Frederick decided to branch out into the world of cinema. He became involved in a business venture in Glasgow with Samuel and then took the bold step of moving to Ireland to become one of the early pioneers of cinema there. On 22nd February 1912, Frederick opened The Panopticon in High Street, Belfast. It was listed as a cinema and waxworks with a museum in the city directory, offering various entertainments just like the original Panopticon at the Tron in Glasgow. It was a relatively small cinema with seating for approximately 350, but it proved popular with the cinema-going public. When it opened, it was described by one newspaper as a "cosy picture theatre" but was a force to be reckoned with thanks to the enterprising manager, Mr Frederick Stewart. All went well with this venture for some years until 1924, when he was forced to close the cinema and put it up for auction due to ill health. A short time later, Frederick was discovered drowned in a stream on the outskirts of Belfast.

Mr Baily:
There was no Mr "Baily" connected to either Samuel, waxworks, circuses, fairgrounds, or entertainment. However, there are two possible candidates, each with a link to Samuel, as they both had their business on Upper Street and so would have been familiar with his waxworks.
The first candidate is Charles Bailey, the son of Francis Bailey. The Bailey family had been travelling show people for generations, touring with their fair and sideshows around England. For three months every year, Francis Bailey gave up the life of a traveller to manage The World's Fair with his partner, Theophilus Read, at the Agricultural Hall located on Upper Street. The Fair ran from December to February, combining an indoor circus, fairground, sideshows, waxworks, freak shows, conjuring shows, musical entertainments, acrobatic displays, and various exhibitions. When Francis Bailey died, his son, Charles Bailey, took his place. So, it is possible that Charles was at the auction, hoping to acquire some extra props or models for the next World's Fair.
The second candidate is Charles Seymour Bayley, a travelling exhibitor and lecturer of novelties and freaks. He was the superintendent and inspector of the sideshows at Earls Court for several years while employed by Imre Kiralfy. In 1899, while at Earls Court, he was also the manager for the Lion Incubator Infant Company. Incubators were on display with live infants inside them for the paying public to view. In August 1899, he was called to give evidence at an enquiry into the death of a baby which had been on display at Earls Court. Dr Goodman, who gave evidence, stated that the eleven-week-old boy had died due to malnourishment and inflammation of the bowels. The incubator had nothing to do with the direct cause of death, but the incubator's unsuitability no doubt weakened the baby. Between May and August of that year, there had been three infant deaths. The jury returned a verdict of "Natural Death" and attached no blame to the incubator company. Incredibly, Bayley did not let this tragedy affect him in any way whatsoever, for he continued in the employ of the incubator company and took the exhibition to Olympia in December of the same year.

He then joined the Barnum and Bailey Show, where he was employed as a lecturer for "many well-known freaks".

He eventually settled in London after meeting Lionel Bartram. The latter convinced him to manage his London mechanical exhibition shop, which was a mixture of copper-capturing devices and moving waxwork models. Bayley claimed that setting up a rifle range within Bartram's shop at 46 Upper Street was his idea, and in 1901, he became the secretary of the Islington Rifle Association. Then, in 1909, with the roller-skating craze sweeping the country, Bayley landed a very lucrative position as general manager for British Rinkeries Ltd.

So, was it Francis Bailey or Charles Seymour Bayley who attended Samuel's auction?

Mr Bartram:
William Lionel Bartram was born around 1852 in Bristol, although for a while, he claimed he was born in the USA. He began his career as a photographer with studios in Southampton, Portsmouth and the Isle of Wight. He and his wife, Lucy, had three children, and throughout their married life, Bartram changed his career several times. In 1888, he sold his studio in Southampton and opened a house agency business while still keeping his other studios. In May of the same year, he became a member of the St Claire Lodge in Landport but was excluded in November of 1893.
In 1890, Bartram was charged with being drunk in charge of a horse and cart and was called to appear in court. Bartram's Doctor, Dr Emmett, appeared in court and claimed that Bartram was too ill to attend the proceedings and he had confined him to bed.

In 1891, while still maintaining the Portsmouth studio, Bartram had moved into temporary lodgings in South Shields and had become a showman. Between 1891 and 1901, he opened several London mechanical waxwork "shops", including the one on Upper Street. The admission cost was just one penny, making it accessible to working-class audiences. For your penny, you could view moving models such as Anthony and Cleopatra, as well as the notable politicians of the time. Your penny also allowed access to several "Peep Shows", some historical, some beautiful and some naughty. It appears that Bartram moved to London before Samuel, but they were clearly well-known to each other, with Samuel's waxwork shop a few doors down from Bartram's. In an interview, Samuel acknowledges that thanks to the influence of Bartram, he was able to put together his own collection of mechanical models. In 1901, while still owning his Penny Gaffs, Bartram became the owner of the Shakespeare Hotel in Sittingbourne, Kent. The family lived in Sittingbourne for several years before moving to Blackpool, where Bartram opened his "Wonderland" attraction. At the auction, Bartram bought the models of Dick Turpin and Edgar Edwards (a triple murderer), intending to add to his shop on Upper Street. Perhaps he was already putting together a collection for his new amusements in Blackpool.

Mr Adams:
David Adams was born around 1859 in Scotland and was a waxwork exhibition proprietor. David and his siblings worked with their mother in her travelling waxwork show around Scotland, England and Wales. The family travelled and toured the country, securing long-term engagements. In 1877, while in Swansea, David Adams appeared in court charged with allowing music in his waxwork exhibition without a licence. A young boy was inside the premises playing a barrel organ, and people were paying 2d to enter the waxwork shop. The music attracted a crowd of people who blocked the pavement outside, and many people complained. The mayor explained that several Tradesmen had complained to him because they could not gain access to their business premises because of the obstruction. The police sergeant who attended the scene admitted that Mr Adams stopped the music immediately after being told that it was inappropriate. One of the waxwork displays was that of the murderer Wainwright and the Whitechapel Tragedy. Mr Adams was not convicted of any crime but, "the Bench" had something to say on the matter before his release:

"...This kind of semi-public entertainment is very undesirable for this borough. It is a great breach of propriety to carry such a brutalising exhibition in a place like this and could only have but one tendency, a mischievous tendency. The sooner you discontinue these exhibitions the better. Why should you exhibit one of the greatest brutes that ever walked the face of this earth? We do not intend to convict you this morning and give you the benefit of the doubt suggested by learned counsel. If you wish to exhibit waxworks you must do so with order and decorum. We advise you to drop the music and the Wainwright exhibition.
(The Cardiff Times & South Wales Weekly News 1877)

For several years, the Adams family exhibited in the Briggate area in Leeds and opened in Redcar, Manchester and London before opening a permanent exhibition in Newcastle. The Newcastle exhibition was known as the "Tussaud's of the North" because the displays and exhibitions were so up to date. In 1901, David Adams went to London to buy the latest mechanical models for Newcastle. He purchased a tableau of Queen Victoria lying in state and paid 2500 French francs for the piping bullfinch from the Paris exhibition. Once back in Newcastle, Adams set up his own Paris exhibition, lit up by electricity, with over a hundred mechanical models, pictures and waxwork models. It was no surprise then that he was at the auction, no doubt on the lookout for new models for his own exhibition.

Mr Baines:
Ernest Gambart Baines was an exhibition proprietor and showman. He was the son of Clementina Baines, a travelling waxwork show owner who had toured England and France with Madame Tussaud. The Baines family toured the country with their exhibition show. In 1881, both Clementina and Ernest toured Yorkshire with two separate shows. After Clementina died in 1890, Ernest took over and expanded the business. When he opened his Royal Waxworks in Oxford, Ernest included a variety of entertainment and waxwork displays. In 1896, he placed an advert asking for novelties and freaks to apply for a position with his show in Manchester, making it clear that only respectable people need apply.

In the early 1900s, Ernest moved to Scarborough and bought the public swimming baths building for £4250, where he installed his waxworks exhibition while keeping the baths open during the summer season. His Mechanical and Musical Promenade show claimed to have the best mechanical models in all of England. The show included a Haunted House, The Execution, The Fortune Telling Fairy and The Dying Child. In 1913, Ernest gifted a motor fire engine to the town of Scarborough at the cost of £1,200. A display was given outside the Grand Hotel for the general public and local dignitaries, followed by the mayor's luncheon for the Watch Committee.

Mr Tussaud:
The name Tussaud is synonymous with waxwork models, and much has been written about the family. Louis Tussaud was the great-grandson of Madame Tussaud and was born in 1867 in Marylebone, one of fourteen children. He married his first cousin, Minnie Frances Tussaud, and had two children together. Louis Tussaud had been brought up in the family business, learning modelling skills passed down through the generations. When he was twenty years old, his terracotta bust of George Grossmith, a popular comic actor, was displayed in the London Art Society Exhibition. In 1888, Tussaud's were forced to set up a limited company, which eventually led to the original company being dissolved, and in 1889, Tussaud's was sold to a syndicate of businessmen. The new company appointed Louis Tussaud's brother as artistic director, which caused a division within the family. It wasn't long before Louis started out on his own. In January 1890, he announced his intention to open his own exhibition on Shaftesbury Avenue in London. He promised that his show would be like no other in London and would be of the highest moral standards. Meanwhile, Madame Tussaud & Company obtained an injunction that restrained Louis Tussaud from registering his new company under the name of Louis Tussaud Limited because it was likely to mislead the public into the belief that the new company was related to the already established Madame Tussaud's exhibition.

The Shaftesbury Avenue plans fell through, but undaunted, Louis opened his show of over 400 portrait models on Regent Street on Christmas Eve to very positive reviews. However, the "moral standards" which had been promised obviously didn't include or apply to the Chamber of Horrors, which took up the whole length of the ground floor where "gruesome curiosities from all around the world" would be on display. Louis had installed several murder scenes in all their distasteful detail, including a tableau of Mrs Mary Pearcey. She was hanged for the murder of her lover's wife and child the day before Louis opened his exhibition. The new waxwork show was an instant success with Londoners, but it wasn't to last. Less than six months after opening, on 20th June 1891, the waxwork exhibition went up in smoke. The entire contents of the building, including all of the wax models, were destroyed by fire. The cause of the fire was never established, but it appears to have started in the Chamber of Horrors at Mrs Pearcey's display. The total cost of damage was estimated at around £18,000, and Louis claimed it would take approximately six months to remould the wax models. Louis was able to recreate 200 of his models, and in March 1892, starting at the Leinster Hall in Dublin, he began a six-month tour of Ireland. He then spent the next eight years touring around the country with his exhibition show. While the show was a huge success with audiences, it wasn't all plain sailing for Louis, and it wasn't long before he was in court in what would become a drawn-out landmark case.

Louis had secured an engagement at the Winter Gardens in Birmingham when, in January 1894, John Monson arrived at the show to complain that a likeness of him had been placed in the exhibition without his consent. (John Monson had been on trial in Edinburgh for murder in the notorious Ardlamont Mystery, where a verdict of not proven was given.) But Monson had an ulterior motive for his complaint. He informed Tussaud's manager that the Madame Tussaud Company in London had offered him a large sum of money for the privilege of exhibiting his likeness. He wanted to know if Mr Louis Tussaud would also be prepared to provide him with financial payment. Louis Tussaud was not prepared to offer any money whatsoever, and Monson left the building, determined that the wax likeness would not remain on view to the public. The news of Monson's visit soon got out and caused quite a sensation. So began a very long, drawn-out, complicated court case as Monson took out actions against both the Madame Tussaud Company and Louis Tussaud Limited. It took a year before the libel trial was eventually heard in the law courts in London on 28th January 1895. Several published accounts of the trial go into minute detail of the events as they unfolded in the courtroom. The daily newspapers followed the proceedings closely as this was to become a landmark case that established the principle of "libel by innuendo" for the first time. The jury took around fifteen minutes to reach a verdict in favour of Monson. However, Monson's victory was somewhat short-lived as he was awarded just one farthing (a quarter of a penny) in damages and made to pay his own costs. Louis Tussaud was instructed to remove Monson's wax model from his exhibition. In the years following this court case, Louis Tussaud continued to travel extensively around the country with his waxwork show, including the exhibition at Alexandra Palace in 1898, which caused much grief for Mr Stiff and Samuel. Around 1900, Louis Tussaud eventually settled in Blackpool, where the exhibition was first shown at the Hippodrome and then the south shore before finally locating to the Central Promenade. Given that Louis was a skilled wax modeller and artist, it is unlikely that he would have attended Samuel's auction intending to purchase any models. It is more reasonable to assume that he was possibly interested in the fittings and decorations, or perhaps he was simply curious.

Mr Barron:
Clarence Barron was born on 29th January 1874 in Norfolk, the son of Leberana Gray and George Barron. In 1898, he married Rose Bonnett, his first cousin and they had five boys together. The Barron family was descended from a line of traders, shop dealers and shopkeepers. The Grays and Bonnetts were both Romany travelling families. Leberana Gray came from a family of travelling musicians who toured around England performing at fairs and circus grounds. Clarence's wife, Rose Bonnet, was the daughter of Keomi Gray, which made Keomi his aunt and his mother-in-law.

Keomi was famous in her day and was well known within Romany society. Frederick Sandys (born Anthony Frederick Augustus Sands 1829 – 1904) was an artist and friend of Dante Rossetti. He had a relationship with Keomi Gray for many years when she became his muse and featured in many of his Pre-Raphaelite works. They had four children together before the relationship ended. Keomi then married Charles Bonnett, a travelling horse dealer and had three daughters together: Ellen, Rose and Florence. Clarence Barron began his career working as a cycle manufacturer in his father's business in Upper Street, Islington. After 1891, Clarence's father opened a shop on Brompton Road, where he traded as a general dealer. Clarence followed his father to Brompton Road and opened a jewellery shop that also sold automated machines. But Clarence was soon to discover the world of waxworks, and by 1901, he was exhibiting a show in Great Yarmouth, but unfortunately, this show and Clarence's actions landed him in court. He was summonsed for using a vehicle to display advertisements without the Corporation's consent. Clarence was running "a heterogeneous exhibition, and in the cellar, there was a wretched exhibition supposed to represent the various phases of the Yarmouth murder." The vehicle in question was advertising this part of the exhibition. One witness saw the American four-wheeled Bogey being driven around the town in the morning by a woman and a youth in the afternoon. According to a newspaper report at the time, "The defendant made capital out of the display of human life in its worst possible features and showed determination to make a permanent display of the exhibition. The Chief Constable and Magistrates wanted to keep Yarmouth pure and free from that which was demoralising to the town, and it was for this reason that the case was brought." The Chief Constable had already cautioned Clarence Barron about the advertisement, but Clarence ignored the warning and continued to drive the advertising cart around the town. Clarence objected to the remarks made about his waxworks as they had no bearing on the offence he was charged with. The Magistrates informed him that they were sorry that he had brought such a discreditable exhibition to their town. Clarence was fined twenty shillings plus costs or faced a jail term of one month. Not put off by his court appearance, this was the start of Clarence's career in amusement catering, which turned into a whole family affair involving his father and brothers. No doubt Clarence bought the "Throne Room" display from Samuel's auction to add to his stock of models for his exhibition show.

Mr Pickard:
Albert Ernest Pickard was born in Bradford in 1874, the son of an innkeeper. He was a showman, entrepreneur, exhibitor, property owner, businessman, millionaire, cinema owner and definitely an eccentric. As a travelling showman, he toured around England before spending some years in London. Then, in 1904, he went to Glasgow and is perhaps best known for buying Fell's Waxworks at the Trongate in Glasgow, then purchasing the Britannia Music Hall and renaming it The Panopticon, where in 1906, a sixteen-year-old Stan Laurel made his stage debut.

Much has been written about the life and times of Albert Ernest Pickard. He wasn't always popular within business circles, as his quirky sense of humour and outlandish publicity stunts were considered to be nothing but attention-seeking acts. However, he was much loved by Glaswegians, who were entertained by his outlandish behaviour and crazy antics. At the time of the auction, Pickard had finished travelling around Essex and Kent before settling in London as a proprietor of shooting galleries. In 1901, he was involved in a disturbing accident which resulted in the death of a young boy: The coroner for East London held an enquiry into the circumstances surrounding the death of 14-year-old George Earl, who was fatally shot at one of Pickard's shooting galleries. The boy's mother gave evidence to the enquiry and explained that she had last seen her son, who was deaf and dumb when he left for school at 9.30 on Friday morning. William Gibson, aged 14 and employed by Pickard to look after the shooting range on Victoria Dock Road, stated that he heard a shot which came from the saloon. When he got there, he found George Earl lying on the floor, bleeding, with a rifle beside him. Gibson explained that he had placed the guns and a box of cartridges on the counter earlier that morning, ready for business at 10 o'clock. A. E Pickard, the gallery owner, said, "The deceased was known as 'The Dummy' and was very troublesome to all the shopkeepers and always in mischief." A verdict of death from misadventure was given.

Unsurprisingly, in 1901, there were no health and safety precautions or regulations for shooting galleries. There is so much that is so wrong about both the situation and the inquest. Apart from the young boy's death, the most disturbing thing is how insensitively Pickard referred to the boy when giving his statement to the coroner. There appears to be no remorse or compassion on the part of Pickard, and his claim that the boy was "always in mischief" makes it sound as if he is implying that such an accident is inevitable. I can't imagine the distress and heartbreak of the boy's mother, which is unimaginable, having to sit at the inquest and listen to the insults from Pickard, who seems to have had a darker, hidden side.

In 1904, his wife filed for divorce on the grounds of cruelty. In the divorce petition, Caroline Pickard gave dates and places with details of physical abuse. She claimed that the first incident occurred five years after their marriage, by which time they had moved to Glasgow. She was pregnant with their fourth child when Pickard struck her on the face, causing her mouth to bleed and kicked her in the stomach. On one occasion, Caroline claimed Pickard kicked her about her body so severely that she lost consciousness.

We shall never know what went on behind those closed doors, but the divorce was never granted, and Caroline stayed in the marriage until sometime around 1925, after which she and Pickard led separate lives. Caroline remained in Glasgow until her death in 1953. But strangely, there is a newspaper report from The Dumfries and Galloway Standard in 1916, which claims that the wife of Albert Pickard, Glasgow Music Hall Proprietor, was granted a divorce in the Court of Session with an allowance of £1000 per annum. Evidence presented in court showed that Pickard had become infatuated with a young girl who worked in his office, and he had stayed with her at Turnberry and Dumfries. This has to be incorrect, for there is no divorce record for the Pickards. When Pickard attended Samuel's auction, he was running his shooting galleries in London, but this was the year before Pickard moved to Glasgow, so perhaps he was hoping to accumulate stock for his new business.

Mr Balls:
In fact, Mr Balls was Alf Ball, born in Hull in 1864, the son of a travelling auctioneer. Initially, he followed his father into the same business, travelling around England until his marriage to Elizabeth (Lily) Cannard in 1882. After his marriage and with financial help from his parents, Alf and Lily started up their own shooting gallery. Over time, they added other games and amusements, travelling around fairs and markets.

Alf was also a very successful amateur boxer who eventually became the middleweight champion of England. He famously challenged the World Champion, Peter Jackson and the fight lasted for forty rounds, even though Alf fought most of the match with a broken arm from an injury sustained in an early round. Alf then created "Professor Ball and School of Boxers", which appeared at all the major fairgrounds and Circus events around England. At one point, he even introduced a boxing lion into the act, which caused a huge sensation at the time. He later introduced "Professor Ball's Midgets" as a sideshow attraction to his shooting saloon. He exhibited the world's smallest married couple for a season at Earl's Court in London under the direction of Imre Kiralfy.

By 1895, Alf was travelling on the same fairground circuits as Francis and Charles Bailey, and he had extended his show to include swing boats and roundabout attractions. Alf was a very shrewd businessman, and when he saw the popularity of moving picture shows introduced to the fairground circuit by Randall Williams, Alf saw this as the next step for him. By 1897, he was on tour with a moving picture show called "The Great American Bioscope Animated Pictures". In 1899, he brought his bioscope exhibition show to Oxford at the St. Giles Fair. This was such a success that by 1902, Alf had put together an efficient show with a staff of operators, photographers and electricians.

His "Royal Bioscope and Theatre of Varieties" had its own traction engine and electric light installation, which toured fairgrounds via the railways in the summer months. In addition, he purchased the Empire Theatre in Maidenhead, where he presented his bioscope exhibitions during the winter months. However, Alf wasn't prepared to give up his love of boxing entirely. Even though he was busy assembling his bioscope show, he had found time to open a boxing ring sideshow in Upper Street, less than a five-minute walk from Samuel's waxworks. Even though there was accommodation above the Upper Street shop, Alf and his family lived in caravans situated on Denmark Street.

He was a very well-respected gentleman within the community of showmen, mainly due to his kindness and consideration towards others, often helping those who found themselves in financial difficulty. The Mitcham Charter Fair was a regular venue for Alf, and in 1906, the Conservators of Mitcham Common applied to the Secretary of State for the abolition of the Fair. Mitcham Fair was held on a triangular-shaped piece of waste ground that sat in the middle of the town. Since the time of Queen Elizabeth I, a fair had been held under a charter on that piece of ground. The Lords of the Manor originally granted the charter to the Lee family. Later, it came into the possession of Francis Bailey (father of Charles Bailey, who also may have attended Samuel's auction). When Francis Bailey died, ownership of the charter became the property of his widow, who sold it to the Conservators of Mitcham Common. As a result, the Conservators issued notices that no showmen, caravans, booths or attractions would be allowed on the Green.

The members of the Showmen's Guild, of which Alf was an active member, were quick to raise objections and petitioned the Secretary of State for the right to representation. They organised a public protest meeting on the fairground at Alf Ball's exhibition. Alf placed an advert in The Era newspaper on 11th August, inviting people to attend the protest meeting to defend the rights and privileges of the people of Mitcham and their ancient Fair. In defiance of the notice served and under Alf's direction, showmen covered the whole of Mitcham Green with their engines, caravans, shows and attractions. Even though there was much local support for the continuance of the Fair, Alf and three other showmen were issued with injunctions, prohibiting them from occupying their usual places on the ground. By 1907, a total of forty-five showmen had been issued with injunctions. Alf was hailed as a champion and a hero who fought for the rights of all showmen. Much correspondence between the Guild of Showmen and the Conservators ensued. The Guild tried to reach a compromise, but the Conservators refused to enter into negotiations.

The upshot of this was that other showmen continued to set up their Fair at Mitcham year after year on the disputed land. But, because of the injunction, Alf and the others were unable to exhibit in their usual place. However, they secured a pitch on privately owned land at the end of London Road. Unfortunately for Alf, he was charged with causing an obstruction and was fined £16 plus costs. This state of affairs went on until 1911, when a compromise was reached, resulting in the management of the Fair being leased to the showmen.

The Mitcham upset didn't stop Alf from continuing the expansion of his travelling bioscope show. At the cost of £5000, Alf had bought a brand-new picture palace from M. Gavioli of Paris. It was probably one of the first picture palaces on wheels in England and possibly the biggest, with the front of the organ measuring 55 feet and the palace itself 80 feet deep. In July 1910, Alf had taken his show to the fairground at Tilbury Docks in Essex when disaster struck. There was a tremendous thunderstorm in the middle of the night, and lightning struck the picture palace. By the time the fire brigade arrived, the damage was done, and the fire was so fierce that the entire palace burnt to the ground. The only thing to escape the flames was Alf's living caravan, which he had parked a little distance away from the show.

Alf was not insured. He was left with nothing. Undaunted and ever resilient, he turned up at Mitcham Fair a few weeks later with a tent which he pitched on the private ground at London Road. He received a rapturous welcome from both showmen and townsfolk. On the Sunday evening, the showmen held their Sunday service in Alf's tent. Alf Ball died in Romford in 1926.

After these legendary characters had attended Samuel's sale of the Upper Street Waxworks, the doors were closed for the last time in August, and Samuel was left to concentrate on his other business projects. It is unclear if he was still the proprietor of his two other variety shops, but he was still travelling around the country with his mobile exhibitions. The travelling show was vitally crucial to Samuel because it was, in fact, a cover for a double life which he had been living for some time. Unfortunately for him, Jessie Rose was about to uncover the secret, which would change their lives forever. In November 1903, Samuel was summoned to court on a charge of desertion.

Jessie Rose's solicitor, Mr Ricketts, explained that the couple had been married for nearly 20 years and had recently run a business together at Upper Street. However, upon finding a love letter written by her husband to a well-known female owner of a waxwork show, Mrs Burnette travelled to Northampton in search of her husband, who had an exhibition there. She waited three days before her husband finally appeared. Unable to offer any reasonable explanation for his absence, she challenged him about the letter. His only response was that it was unfortunate that he had been found out and made promises that it would never happen again. Unsatisfied and suspicious of her husband's easy promises, she returned to Northampton at a later date to find her husband absent again. On the 1st of August, she packed up the exhibition and returned to London with it. Mr Burnette wrote to his wife telling her he had 'done with her' and paid her £1 to look after all six children. Unable to survive on such a paltry amount, Mrs Burnette was forced to enter the workhouse at Wolverhampton. On her departure from the workhouse, Mrs Burnette left the children with her husband. The solicitor then informed the court that Mr Burnette had savings of £15 each week and, since his summons, had sent his wife £2. Mr Warburton, for the defendant, claimed that this was an inaccurate representation of Mr Burnette's financial affairs. Indeed, Mr Burnette had left his wife with furniture to the value of £250 and stated that Mrs Burnette had been very unkind to her husband.

When questioned by the judge, Jessie Rose declared that she no longer wanted her children because her husband was never at home; he didn't know the children, and it was time he knew them. In reply, Mr Burnette declared that he was fond of the children, one being just a baby and that he would look after them. An order was made by agreement.

So, Samuel had been found out. For years, he had been having an affair with Emily D'Arc, daughter of Lambert and Ann Jane D'Arc. It had been an easy secret to keep because of the time Samuel spent away from home. He had also been running a branch of his French Glass, Distorting Mirrors and Parisian Novelties out of St. Mary Street in Cardiff, the exact location as the D'Arc's Waxwork exhibition. This gave him the perfect excuse to visit Emily D'Arc on a regular basis.

Samuel's absences had made things impossibly difficult for Jessie Rose, who was left on her own with six young children and very little money coming in. The workhouse was a last resort, and she wouldn't have gone there had there been any other solution to the situation she found herself in. But what about the children? The court report doesn't make it clear what happened to the children. Did they go into the workhouse too, or had Jessie Rose left them with her family? It is more than likely that the children did indeed go into the workhouse because, by 1891, Jessie Rose's parents had separated and would have been unable to offer any support. By 1891, her father was a pauper in Bath workhouse, where he remained until he died in 1901. Her mother moved to London and, in 1901, was working as a nurse, living with Jessie Rose's eldest brother, George. Unfortunately, by 1911, she, too, ended up a pauper in the Hammersmith workhouse.

How had it come to this? What had Samuel done with the money raised from the auction? Had he given it to his mother? Had he got into financial difficulty himself with some new business venture? Did he have debts that Jessie Rose was unaware of, or had he kept the money to support his new life with Emily D'Arc? How could Samuel have ignored the situation that he had left his wife and children in? In court, he had said he was "done" with Jessie Rose. It is one thing for a marriage to break down, but it is another matter entirely to be uncaring for the welfare of your children. To neglect your wife and children to the extent that the only option was the workhouse was a profound and far-reaching mistake on Samuel's part. This did not reflect well upon him, and he must surely have been aware of the damage this would do to his hard-earned respect and reputation as a businessman within the entertainment world.

After the court case, with Samuel accepting custody of the children, there is some evidence to show that he did indeed have the children with him. With the sale of the Upper Street waxworks, Samuel was now free to turn his attention to travelling wherever he wished, but it couldn't have been easy on the road with six children to care for. Early in 1904, he was working in Lancashire when his youngest son, Sam Redvers Rendell, died there aged just two.

1904 continued to be a miserable year for Samuel. In December, he was back in court at Jarrow on a charge of pretending to tell fortunes, to which he pleaded not guilty. Samuel opened an exhibition shop displaying mechanical models, distorted mirrors, and four fortune-telling machines on Ellison Street. Sergeant Binns and police constable Butler each visited the exhibition on different nights, and both men gave evidence in court against Samuel. Sergeant Binns went into great detail about how, for a penny, each machine gave him two printed slips of paper, which foretold of future events. He also described a machine that pretended to give a picture of his future wife, mother-in-law, or first baby. Samuel's defence was that these machines had been part of his show for the last fourteen years and had never run foul of the law in all that time. He pleaded ignorance to having broken the law and explained that the machines were simply humorous parts of his show as a card marked 'Fun for the Million' was displayed above each machine. However, the magistrates ruled that they were sufficiently convinced that the machines did pretend to tell fortunes, and as such, an offence against the law had been committed. Samuel was ordered to pay court costs, including those of Victor, his son, and Harry Harrison, his assistant, who had been charged with assisting at the machines. The magistrates also prohibited Samuel from using the machines again.

Samuel's time in London was well and truly over. By 1905, he was looking for new work, including any managerial or responsible position. With his business sold and his marriage finished Samuel spent the next couple of years travelling with his exhibition before leaving England and moving to settle in Glasgow with Emily D'Arc.

CHAPTER TWELVE

AN ABANDONED BABY

(Emily D'Arc, image credit: Ian Armstrong.)

Lambert D'Arc was a waxwork modeller from Rheims in France and had been invited to England by the Tussaud family to work for them, but he quickly set up on his own, travelling around the country. In 1865, Lambert married Ann Jane North, the daughter of a Bath publican. Together, they had six children: George, Emily, Petronella, Mary, William John and Ethelreda.

In 1876, Lambert was sentenced to four months hard labour in Belle Vue Prison, Manchester, for keeping a disorderly house and exhibiting lewd tableau vivants. (Tableaux vivants were nothing better than peep shows for customers willing to pay extra money. Naked women were on display as objects of art, and proprietors got away with this as long as the women remained motionless.) In addition, five ballerinas arrested at the show were each fined five shillings.

The D'Arc's early years were spent in Dublin, where Lambert performed his lavish shows at the Rotunda for four years before eventually settling in Cardiff. In 1884, Mons. D'Arc's Grand Waxwork Exhibition was opened at 90 St Mary Street. Its rooms boasted tableaux of the rich and famous of the day, theatre rooms for visiting performers, a chamber of horrors and the macabre, as well as freak exhibition showrooms.

Lambert's waxwork marionette shows were unlike anything that audiences had seen before, and it wasn't long before he was in great demand by entertainment agents. Lambert accepted work in Europe and beyond, taking all six children with him. The show had become a family affair, with the children all playing a part in the performance. In 1890, Lambert and the children embarked upon a tour of South Africa while Ann Jane stayed in Cardiff, managing their exhibition theatre. After South Africa, the show moved on to India and then a grand tour of Australia. Unfortunately, Lambert became seriously ill and was sent to a hospital in Sydney, leaving the children to continue with the show on their own. All was going well, and the children had just heard that their father had left the hospital and was on his way to join them when disaster struck. While performing in Cooktown, the stage caught fire and destroyed all the scenery, props and almost all 350 marionettes. The entire stock, which was valued at £3000, was uninsured.

MONS. D'ARC'S WAXWORK MARIONETTES ENTERTAINMENT

Instead of returning to Cardiff with the children, which would have been the easy option, Lambert decided to rebuild his show. After replacing and reassembling, the tour continued to Thursday Island, a small island located in the Torres Strait, off the north coast of Queensland. This is where a final disaster struck. Lambert D'Arc died on 28 June 1893 at the Douglas Hotel, Thursday Island.

Surely now was the time to return to Cardiff and settle into the family business there? But no, five months after the death of Lambert, the D'Arc's were performing in Singapore before moving on to Hong Kong and then Japan the following year. Eventually, the decision was taken to return to the UK via Hong Kong. Unfortunately, Hong Kong was quarantined due to cholera, so the siblings travelled to Vladivostok instead. Once Hong Kong was declared free, the D'Arc's returned, but they travelled to Calcutta instead of returning to Britain. This was thanks to a booking made by their new manager, Ernest Clitherow, who had married one of Lambert's daughters, Petronella (Nellie) D'Arc, in Hong Kong. After Calcutta, it was on to Bombay, and then Clitherow secured bookings in South Africa for most of 1895.

According to an interview with Emily's brother, William, the siblings toured for eight and a half years after the death of their father before going their separate ways. After the unfortunate death of Nellie from cholera, Emily and Ethel sold their shares in the business and returned to Wales, where they helped their mother run the Cardiff waxworks exhibition show.

But what of Emily D'Arc herself? While the family toured Australia and the Far East, Emily was in charge of the elaborate and luxurious wardrobe and props for the marionettes. Apart from being part of the family business, very little is known of her early years.

However, a tragic, heartbreaking, and disturbing incident occurred while Emily was in Australia, one that doesn't put Emily in a very favourable light. In 1892, while the D'Arcs were touring Australia, Emily dropped out of the show and stayed in Melbourne, while the rest of the family moved on to tour the coastal cities of Queensland. There appears to have been a disagreement between Emily and her father, with Emily refusing to speak to him.

Emily had stayed in Melbourne because she was pregnant. She gave birth to a son, William Henry, in June 1892. His birth was registered in the Carlton district of Melbourne, with Emily D'Arc listed as the mother, but there was no father named on the document.

With the family about to embark on the next stage of their tour, Lambert dispatched his other daughter, Mary, to Melbourne, who was able to convince Emily to rejoin the show. Emily returned from Melbourne to continue the tour, leaving her baby son behind with a nurse in Melbourne. Lambert certainly knew of Emily's situation, but the question is, was the decision to leave the baby Emily's alone or did her father put so much pressure on her that she felt she had no choice in the matter? Did Emily plan to return for the baby when the tour ended, or was there never any intention to acknowledge him? It may have been the latter, as suggested in a letter written by Emily's mother to the Melbourne Police, which only came to light in recent years:

Victoria rooms,
Cardiff
8 June
1893

Dear Sir
I received a letter from Mrs Snudden, 13 Henty Street Richmond Victoria – last Tuesday respecting a baby (boy) which she is nursing for my daughter Emily D'Arc – and in her letter she tells me that she is unable to keep it any longer – on account of not having been paid for some considerable time past, that the amount now owing her is £9 odd and her Husband has had no work for many months she tells me that she will be obliged to give him up to the Police as a neglected child – which would mean exposure and disgrace for my unfortunate daughter as none knows anything about it but herself and Father – I mean in our family my idea, and desire in addressing you is, if such is done – could it be done in a quiet manner, without exposure – if so I should be more than glad – for her sake – There is a House of Nazareth at Ballerat – and who would take him in for a small sum per week – I am in communication and shall be in a few days – with that Institution – Through a letter of introduction from the Good sisters here at Cardiff – to whom I am well known, and am one of their Benefactresses – if the child could be placed there quietly and through your kind influence I shall be most glad – he is Baptised a Roman Catholic as we all are – and Nazareth House is a Roman Catholic House in there he would be right – will you kindly do me the favour of assisting perhaps officially in this matter – and any expenses incurred, please inform me – and I will at once communicate with you – allow me to apologise in troubling you – and hoping to hear from you at your earliest convenience – I may mention that I have today forwarded Mrs Snudden a little money on the behalf of the baby £20.

I beg to remain yours respectfully Ann Jane D'Arc MADAME D'ARC PROPRIETRESSD'ARC'S GRAND WAXWORKS CARDIFF.

Emily had made financial arrangements with Mrs Snudden to look after the baby. Was this a lump sum, or was it a weekly arrangement? With Emily travelling across Australia, how easy would it have been for regular payments to be made to the childminder? Had Emily planned for this to be a temporary arrangement or a more permanent one? Although we don't have all the facts or know the full circumstances regarding Emily's situation or who the baby's father was, it is clear from the letter that there was never any intention to retrieve the baby and bring him back to the U.K. Instead, Emily's mother wanted the whole thing hushed up, afraid of the scandal and disgrace that it would bring upon them. Furthermore, Ann Jane D'Arc's letter was dated a year after the birth of the baby, which means William Henry had been separated from his mother, Emily, for a year.

In the letter, Emily's mother is keen to point out that she is well-known to the nuns in Cardiff and that she is generous with her monetary donations. As a successful businesswoman, Ann Jane D'Arc would have relished her role as a benefactress to the convent and considered it her moral and Catholic duty to support the nuns in their good works. However, some may have thought that her Christian duty would have served her better had she found a way to welcome her grandson into the family. William Henry D'Arc had become a ward of the state in Victoria in 1892. The date of the letter is interesting because just two weeks later, on 28 June, Lambert D'Arc died on Thursday Island on 28 June.

Emily was back in Wales by 1901, by which time Samuel had established his business in London. With Jessie Rose in charge of the Upper Street waxworks, Samuel was free to travel the country with his show, and that's when Samuel and Emily began their love affair.

Samuel left the London scandal behind him and started a new chapter of his life in Glasgow with Emily. Frederick Rendell Burnette was able to pass Emily off as his wife. She was often referred to as "Madame Burnette", and the myth of her being of French birth was established. Having a French father, Emily was probably a fluent French speaker, and it would have been an easy illusion to maintain. Emily had, in fact, been born in Worcester.

With the discovery of his affair and the selling up of his businesses in London, Samuel needed a fresh start. With his experience of having performed all around the country, he could have chosen many other locations. Was it fate, luck, timing, or a conscious decision to make a new life in Scotland? It was far enough away from London, and he had reliable connections in Scotland, which probably made him choose to move to Dundee in the summer of 1905. There, he opened an exhibition shop at Overgate, where he stayed until the end of the year.

> *The Electric Wonders under the management of Mr F R Burnette is at present on view at Dundee and is receiving splendid patronage.*
> Music Hall and Theatre Review 7 July 1905.

The show continued to receive good reviews, but Samuel was looking for bigger audiences, and so he moved to Aberdeen thanks to his acquaintance with James Walter Humber. Humber was a contemporary of Samuel who started his career as a conjurer, ventriloquist and marionette master performing under the stage name of Professor Rebmuh. He toured the same performing circuits as Samuel, where they probably first met. They certainly knew each other during the London years. Samuel became good friends with Frederick Stewart, who owned a waxwork exhibition on Upper Street, close to Samuel's waxwork shop, and James Walter Humber was Stewart's manager. Humber later went into partnership with Stewart, and together, they opened the Edinburgh Waxworks on the High Street. Humber then opened a shop in Leith before moving to Aberdeen, where he opened a waxwork variety shop on George Street. Samuel turned up at Humber's and exhibited his mechanical models there until early 1906.

> *Several new French working models have been added to Burnett's Electrical Wonders in Aberdeen. These include a cornet soloist, who plays solos and faithfully depicts life in all his movements. This show will be transferred to Glasgow in a week or two.*
> (Music Hall and Theatre Review 9 February 1906)

Perhaps initially, Samuel saw the Glasgow exhibition as just another paying engagement. He was already familiar with the entertainment world in Glasgow, and he must have realised the potential for making a new life there for himself and Emily. By 1906, Glasgow's entertainment scene was thriving. A. E Pickard's Exhibition Museum at the Trongate was already popular with audiences, and on Argyle Street, Herbert Crouch's Wonderland was already well established as the venue for waxworks, human freaks, automata, mechanical models and moving pictures.

Herbert Crouch was born in London in 1843, the son of a footman. He was employed at Crystal Palace for a short time before he put together his own travelling peep show, which he took all around the country, eventually arriving in Scotland during the Glasgow Fair. Crouch must have liked the look of the city because he settled there after the industrial holiday period and opened a shooting range and mechanical exhibition, which ran at the Trongate for several years. He later moved to 137 Argyle Street, where he opened his waxwork exhibition show. "Crouch's Wonderland" became renowned for its freaks and oddities as well as its mechanical and wax models. Herbert Crouch was the first person to show Barnum's famous bearded lady, Annie Jones. "Wonderland" closed in 1912, and Crouch became the owner of Clydebank Picture Palace.

Meanwhile, at Cowcaddens, Frederick Stewart of London and Edinburgh fame had opened a waxwork exhibition shop. Samuel wanted to be part of this world. Pickard, Crouch, and Stewart were already very successful businessmen. They would have been strong competition for Samuel, but he was completely undaunted by this, such was his self-belief, determination, and desire to become successful within the entertainment industry. Frederick Rendell Burnette had arrived in Glasgow, ready to make his mark.

> *WANTED, Novelties and Freaks with good Posters &c., for Glasgow on salary. F Burnette, Manager 273 Argyle Street Glasgow.*
> (The Era, 5 May 1906)

> *WANTED, Good Freaks and Novelties to follow Madame Herculine. Prof Elba, Glennie's Marionettes &. Co, Can book you two months certain. Terms. Salary. Fred Burnette New Permanent Exhibition 273 Argyle Street, Glasgow.*
> (The Era 19 May 1906)

Madame Herculine was a touring weightlifter, athlete, and wrestler, her claim to fame being that she was the world champion heavy-weight lifter of the time. She was often known as the Lady Samson. John Edward Marshall was a joiner by trade who toured the Music Halls as a conjurer under the stage name of Professor Elba. In 1930, he was sentenced to five months in prison for counterfeiting coins. When Detectives searched his lodgings, they found numerous counterfeit coins, including half-crowns, florins, shillings, sixpences, pennies and halfpennies; his collection of coins was described as unique!

One month later, Samuel's business had a new name:

> *WANTED. Good freaks and Novelties, now and future dates. Can book you two months in Scotland. Terms. Salary. The Caledonian Waxwork and Mechanical Wonders. 273 Argyle Street, Glasgow. Proprietor, Fred Burnette.*
> (The Era 2 June 1906)

The following week, Samuel placed another advert in The Era asking for Glennie's Marionettes to wire him at 273 Argyle St for an engagement starting on 18 June. Professor Glennie's Marionettes was a very successful puppeteer company, established in the late 1800s and proved popular with family audiences around the country. Samuel was aiming high to attract the best variety acts for his show. Throughout that first summer season, Samuel placed regular wanted ads in The Era, looking for the variety acts that would attract audiences, including one very specific request for a young lady:

> *WANTED Young Lady about 9st, slight knowledge of Strong Business or other Athletics to assist in Strong Act, shops and halls. Send photo., Saxo, Varieties. 273 Argyle Street Glasgow.*
> (The Era 18 August 1906)

One month later, the business changed its name yet again:

WANTED, Living Freaks and Novelties, nothing too big, 12 weeks certain. The Scottish Novelty Syndicate, 273 Argyle Street Glasgow.
(The Era 8 September 1906)

Samuel's first year at Argyle Street was a great success, but it wasn't until December of that first year that he really established himself as a front-runner within entertainment circles. In July of that year, A. E Pickard had opened his Panocoption and had a waxwork display of human sacrifices at Dahomey. However, Samuel went one better than that and secured a live performing troupe of Dahomey Warriors:

In January 1907, Samuel caused a great sensation in Glasgow when he produced a live show of Dahomey Amazon Warriors at his Novelty Palace in Argyle Street. The crowd of people queuing for the show was so immense that hundreds were turned away, and the police had to manage the crowd and control traffic. There was a special performance on Hogmanay when gifts were exchanged, and speeches were given. Samuel presented Chief Angazza Lobogolo with a solid gold medal, and "Mrs Burnette" presented Princess Gooma with a necklace and earrings. Each warrior received a gift in sterling metal, and gentlemen friends of Samuel and Emily gave the princess six armlets. Samuel was both delighted and surprised to receive an inscribed silver cigarette case, a gift from the warriors and theatre staff. The evening ended with a rousing rendition of "Auld Lang Syne".

This was a real coup for Samuel, proving he had good business and marketing skills. It was also the first Glasgow public reference to "Mrs Burnette," for this was not Jessie Rose, but Emily D'Arc, who was posing as Samuel's wife. Samuel continued building, expanding, and diversifying his business interests in Glasgow and beyond with Emily by his side. Finally, with the Argyle Street business proving a success, he decided to venture into photography. With new technology constantly developing, Samuel saw the potential and opportunities that a career in the industry could offer.

In 1907, one year after opening his waxworks, he opened a shop in Gallowgate, Rothesay. This was the beginning of F R Burnette, Photographer, a business that lasted for many years. By 1909, F. R Burnette had a new studio at 17 East Princes Street, and later, he opened a new studio at 10 Argyll Street and yet another one at Dean Hood Place, all in Rothesay. Rothesay may seem an odd location for Samuel to choose, but like a majority of Glasgow folk at the time, he and Emily would no doubt have visited the resort on one of the Clyde steamers. Ever forward-thinking, he would have seen the location's potential as a moneymaker. Rothesay also had a connection to Samuel's past and present. Frederick Stewart already owned a property in East Princes Street, just a few doors down from Samuel's first studio. Was it because of Stewart that Samuel first visited Rothesay? He evidently liked what he saw, not just in terms of future business opportunities but also on a more personal level.

At the same time as opening the Rothesay studios, Samuel was still very much involved in expanding his city businesses, opening three Glasgow studios, one at 55 Argyle Street, one at 186 Argyle Street and an office and studio at 108 Renfield Street. His first Glasgow studio in Argyle St was initially known as The Lightning Studio. Eventually, all the Glasgow studios became known as "Mr B's" and cleverly bore a Bumblebee trademark logo. In 1909, Samuel and Emily were living in a rented property at 12 Douglas Street, Glasgow, and according to the electoral roll, Samuel was an electrical engineer. The Glasgow studios became a family concern, with Samuel's two sons, Victor and Herbert, as assistant photographers. Victor progressed within the business, becoming a photographer in his own right.

(Business cards from Burnette's collection, image credit: Ian Armstrong.)

In April 1909, Samuel sold off his life-sized mechanical figures and waxwork models. He was done with exhibition shops. Not content with running a chain of photography studios, Samuel entered into a new business venture with Frederick Stewart. They formed The Argyle Amusement Syndicate company and opened a roller-skating rink at 55 Argyle St in Glasgow, no doubt because he saw this as an easy money maker thanks to the skating craze at the time. Samuel engaged A V Gardner as the architect. Gardner was young and relatively inexperienced, having begun his independent practice only the year before. Gardner completed the plans in November 1909.

In a newspaper interview, Samuel claimed that he had purchased the property at 55 Argyle St. This wasn't entirely true and is another example of Samuel misleading people, trying to convince them of his business acumen by talking a good talk. 55 Argyle St belonged to Robert Love Holmes, a bookseller. It contained several shop units with warehouses and stores at the back of the building, which Holmes rented out. Samuel and Frederick had rented property from Holmes on Bunhouse Ground at the back of 55 Argyle St, which consisted of a basement and ground-level halls. Being built of brick and corrugated iron, this rink was merely a conversion of an existing warehouse. Samuel did not own the land or any property at 55 Argyle St, simply the framework of the rink, which was erected either late 1909 or early 1910.

Samuel and Frederick opened their rink on 17 February 1910. It could hold between 300 and 400 skaters, with an overhead alley for learners and trick skating. It was lit by gas and electricity, provided retiring rooms for ladies and gentlemen, and even had a tea - room under the gallery. The floor was made of maple wood, and the skating area covered 18,000 square feet. It was open every day from 10 am to 10.30 pm, with a military orchestra providing all-day music. Although the rink proved popular, it was a very short-lived affair. The roller-skating craze was beginning to wane, and Glasgow audiences were starting to show more interest in moving pictures. However, Samuel and Frederick's venture had been a successful money-making venture.

55 ARGYLE STREET ROLLER RINK

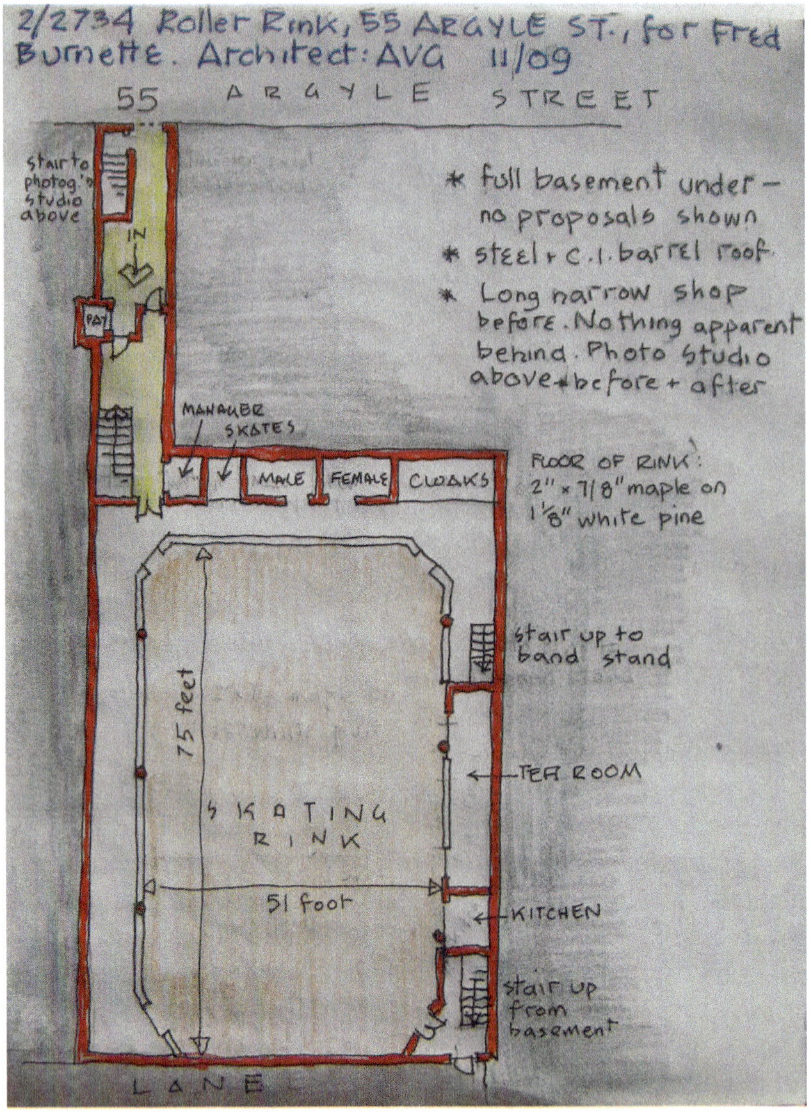
2/2734 Roller Rink, 55 ARGYLE ST., for Fred Burnette. Architect: AVG 11/09
55 ARGYLE STREET
stair to photog.'s studio above
IN
PAY
MANAGER
SKATES
MALE
FEMALE
CLOAKS
* full basement under - no proposals shown
* steel + C.I. barrel roof
* Long narrow shop before. Nothing apparent behind. Photo studio above + before + after
FLOOR OF RINK: 2" × 7/8" maple on 1 1/8" white pine
stair up to band stand
75 feet
TEA ROOM
SKATING RINK
51 foot
KITCHEN
stair up from basement
LANE

(Image credit: Chris Doak.)

ARGYLE STREET ROLLER RINK

FUN ON WHEELS FOR LADIES AND GENTLEMEN.
DAILY SESSIONS. MILITARY BAND.

(Frederick Rendell Burnette, image credit: Peter Lane.)

By 1909, Samuel had become a very successful businessman with well-established photography studios in Glasgow and Rothesay, as well as his roller-skating rink. Samuel and Emily had settled in Glasgow, with Samuel making occasional visits to Rothesay to keep an eye on his business there. But, not content with photographs and roller skates, Samuel was looking for new business projects. Fascinated with all things electrical, mechanical and technological, he wanted to move with the times. Waxwork exhibitions and freak shows had had their day, and people were no longer impressed with parlour tricks and marionettes. Samuel understood that audiences were looking for new experiences that would keep them wanting more. Samuel understood audiences. He was ready to woo them!

The first moving picture was been shown in Scotland in 1896 at the Empire Palace Theatre in Edinburgh, and the first Scottish film was shown at The Skating Palace in Glasgow the same year. This was the new entertainment for people, and, equally important, it was also new employment for the people. This was the future, and Samuel wanted a slice of the action. He was in the right place at the right time.

Before opening their roller rink, Samuel and Frederick had formed The West of Scotland Electric Theatres Ltd company to carry on the business of theatre and music hall proprietors and of electrical engineers and contractors. The company was registered in December 1909, and their office was based at 55 Argyle St. This suggests that before they opened the skating rink, Samuel and Frederick already had plans to open a cinema, and the rink was simply a quick and easy, money-making enterprise. Samuel and Frederick were on the brink of making Scottish cinema history and establishing themselves as pioneers of early cinema in Scotland. On May 12, 1910, their company, "The West of Scotland Theatres Ltd," opened the very first purpose-built cinema in Glasgow.

CHARING CROSS ELECTRIC THEATRE

KINEMACOLOR IS COMING.

(1910 advert, with kind permission of The Daily Record newspaper.)

Charing Cross Electric Theatre on Sauchiehall Street was opened May 12, 1910. Situated in a busy part of Glasgow, close to the exhibition site at Kelvingrove, it was designed by George Arthur Boswell who incorporated the existing frontage of the warehouse which had stood on the site. It had a capacity for a seated audience of around 450. As if opening the first purpose- built cinema wasn't a big enough coup, Samuel and Frederick went one step further. They had managed to secure the sole rights for Kinemacolor in Glasgow. Kinemacolor was the first successful colour motion picture process. Invented by George Albert Smith, it was used commercially from 1908 to 1914. Samuel and Frederick would have been up against serious competition for the exclusive rights and it is hard to know how Samuel pulled this off, but he was a very perceptive, intuitive man when it came to the next big thing in entertainment. This was Samuel reinventing himself again - another example of his progressive, innovative way of thinking. Within a very short time, he had gone form exhibiting freakish wax models on Sauchiehall Street to the proprietor of the first custom-made cinema in Glasgow.

CHARING CROSS ELECTRIC THEATRE.
REVOLUTION IN PORTUGAL.
LAW OF THE WEST (Western Drama).
And All the Latest and Best Pictures.
Unsurpassed for Clearness and Steadiness.
PROGRAMME CHANGED MONDAYS
and THURSDAYS.
OPEN DAILY. 2.30 p.m. until 10.30 p.m.
Admission 6d. Children Half-price until 6.30 p.m.

(1910 advert, with kind permission of The Daily Record newspaper.)

(Charing Cross Electric Theatre, image credit: Bruce Peter.)

A specially invited audience of 300, including many press reporters, attended the opening night when they were presented with a two-part programme. The first featured both comic and dramatic pictures before introducing Kinemacolor for the first time in Scotland. The evening was an instant success, with everyone thoroughly impressed by the colour and detail of the pictures. The following day, Friday 13 May, at twelve noon, The Electric was opened to the public. For audiences who had only seen black-and-white moving images, this was a magical experience. Samuel and Frederick ran continuous programmes throughout the day, and The Electric was so popular that the queue for each showing was several streets long. Days after opening, the management placed apology notices in the press because hundreds of people were turned away daily. A fortnight after opening, the star attraction was a showing of the late King Edward VII's funeral in Kinemacolor when people had to queue for at least an hour to find a seat. It closed briefly in 1912 for a refurbishment and continued to enjoy success with audiences. By 1913, Sauchiehall Street had no less than eight picture theatres, with six of them showing continuous films in competition with The Electric. Crowds at The Electric, however, continued to be four and five people deep. Samuel's company ran The Electric until 29 April 1916. The lease had run out, and he and Frederick chose not to renew it because, by that point, they had both moved on with individual enterprises. It reopened later that year under the management of the Charing Cross Cinema Ltd Company and was renamed simply Charing Cross Cinema. Glasgow boasted 120 cinema halls when it reopened, but it still managed to run successfully until 1926, when it was sold to a Palais de Dance company. It later became the Locarno Ballroom before ending up as a casino.

(Bridgeton Electric, image credit: Travel Lens Photography Collection.)

Samuel and Frederick wasted no time opening their next cinema. The Bridgeton Electric opened on Friday, 18 November 1910, six months after the Charing Cross Electric. George Arthur Boswell was given the contract, but there is no information to say whether this was another purpose-built cinema or a conversion of an existing building, but more than likely the latter. It had a seating capacity of 600 and ran on the same lines as the original Electric, with continuous daily Kinemacolor films and the same cost of admission. With admirable alliteration, the press described it as cosy, comfortable and commodious, with films that were pleasing and palatable to all patrons. It was an instant success with east-end audiences, and much of this was thanks to Willie McGaw, the manager. McGaw, who was in charge of both cinemas, proved to be a very enterprising manager. He commissioned a Celtic v Clyde football match to be filmed, and hundreds of football enthusiasts queued for admission to the cinema.

(1910 advert for Charing Cross and Bridgeton, with kind permission of The Daily Record.)

Samuel and Frederick's association with the Bridgeton Electric didn't last. In 1912, it was taken over by cinema entrepreneur George Green and was known as Green's Picturedrome.

THE ARGYLE ELECTRIC THEATRE

(Sketch of Argyle Electric Theatre, author's own collection.)

Even with two picture houses and exclusive rights to Kinemacolor to their name, Samuel and Frederick were well aware of the stiff competition as Glasgow became caught up in the cinema craze. Two other picture houses opened in Bridgeton that same year and other early cinema proprietors were opening up halls all around Glasgow. While still owners of the West of Scotland Electric Theatres Ltd, Samuel and Frederick created a new company. This was quite a shrewd move on their part. One company sold its assets to the other in order to raise cash and hopefully attract shareholders to invest and, therefore, raise more capital. In 1910, The Argyle Electric Theatre Company Limited was formed:

ARGYLE ELECTRIC THEATRE COMPANY

This Company has been formed for the purpose of acquiring the Halls recently erected by the Vendors on ground leased to them at the back of property forming Nos. 49 to 55 Argyle Street, Glasgow, which are presently used as a Skating Rink, and it is proposed to convert them into an Electric picture Theatre or Amusement Hall. The cost of alterations and fittings will not exceed £1250.

This site is considered one of the best in the city, Argyle Street being the rendezvous of holiday people, who visit the city in large numbers and invariably frequent the places of amusement in the neighbourhood.

The entrance to the Halls forms No. 55 Argyle Street, which will be held, together with the ground on which the Halls stand, on a 13-year lease from Whitsunday 1910, at an annual rent of £300. The Landlord has the right to terminate the lease at the end of the sixth year in the event of the sale of the adjoining property, but in that case, he will pay the Company £100 for each complete year the lease may then have to run. It is believed that Electric Pictures have become as permanent an amusement as the ordinary theatre. These entertainments have been established on the continent and in America for the past 15 years and have enjoyed increasing popularity.

The Vendors are Mr Frederick Rendell Burnette, Photographic Artist, 55 Argyle Street, Glasgow and Mr Frederick Stewart, Exhibition Proprietor, 18 Lothian Street, Edinburgh. They have agreed to make over the Halls, subject to the Landlord's rights under the lease together with their whose rights and interests in the lease for £2000 in cash and £1300 is fully paid Deferred Shares of the Company of which £300 will be paid to the Argyle Amusement Syndicate for services rendered in fully paid Deferred Shares. The fact that the Vendors are willing to take Deferred Shares in part payment of their purchase price shows the confidence they have in the business.

An agreement entered into between Frederick Rendell Burnette, Photographic Artist, 55 Argyle Street, Glasgow and Frederick Stewart, Exhibition Proprietor, Edinburgh of the first part; The Argyle Amusement Syndicate 163 Hope Street, Glasgow for the second part; and James Gray Crawford, 163 Hope Street, Glasgow as Trustee for the Company, of the third part, dated <u>17th June 1910.</u>

Agreement between the said Frederick Rendell Burnette of the one part and the said James Gray Crawford, as Trustee for the Company of the other part under which the first party agrees to serve the Company in the capacity as manager for a period of three years, dated <u>17th June 1910</u>

SHARE CAPITAL £5500

16,800 Cumulative Participating Preference Shares of 5/- each

5200 Deferred Shares of 5/- each

DIRECTORS:

John McMahon, Sheriff Park House, Rutherglen, Provision Merchant, Director of Clyde Football Club Limited.

J.A.D. McLean, 4 Campbell Drive, Queens Park, Glasgow, Merchant, Chairman of Scotland Billiard Company

John C. Oswald, tailor and Outfitter, 170 High Street, Edinburgh

Frederick Stewart, 18 Lothian Street, Edinburgh, Proprietor Stewart's Exhibition, one of the Vendors, will join the Board after Allotment.

ARCHITECT: Albert V. Gardner 164 Bath Street Glasgow.

The Directors are a good indication of the Company and social circles in which Samuel was moving. They were all successful, well-established businessmen:

Clyde Football Club was at rock bottom when John McMahon invested money in it. He was instrumental in the club's rejuvenation and had the foresight to see the potential earnings from greyhound racing at the Shawfield Stadium. He was a club director for many years and was also President of the Scottish Football League. It is widely accepted that the League became a much more powerful and influential body under his management than at any other time. He was a quiet-spoken, well-respected, firm but fair gentleman, and according to his obituary, "There has been no finer gentleman within football and without."

A shoemaker's son, James Archibald Dunlop McLean, started as a commercial traveller but became a partner and managing director of Edgar and Crerar, a bedding manufacturing company with businesses in Glasgow and the north of Scotland.

John Clinkerscales Oswald inherited his father's tailoring business in the High Street, Edinburgh. He was also a partner in James C Smith & Co, Tailors and Clothiers, Edinburgh.

Samuel not only made himself a pile of money from this deal but also agreed to be the manager for a period of three years. The application form for Preference Shares in the Company stated that applicants must be willing to accept less than the number of shares applied for, which implied that there was a great demand for the shares, and applicants may have been disappointed. This prospectus was drawn up in June 1910, and The Argyle Electric Theatre was opened in December of the same year, a mere six-month turnaround.

On the prospectus, A. V. Gardner (who bought 400 shares in the Company) is listed as the project's architect. Several architectural and cinema authorities credit George Arthur Boswell (architect of the first two "Electrics") as the architect of the Argyle Electric Theatre. There is no evidence of a collaboration between the two architects, so something clearly prevented Gardner's involvement in the project.

A.V. Gardner was an independent architect from 1908 until 1912, working from an office in Bath Street, Glasgow. He had graduated from The Glasgow School of Art in 1905, so he was a relatively young man at the time. I suspect that Samuel may have wanted Gardner in on the project because he had been Samuel's original architect on the skating rink at 55 Argyle Street. Gardner's recent commissions had been relatively low-key affairs, mostly small buildings for the Post Office, so perhaps the company's directors wanted a more experienced man for the job. The Argyle Electric Theatre was opened on 24 December 1910 and was an instant success.

ARGYLE ELECTRIC THEATRE.
55 ARGYLE STREET, GLASGOW
(Corner of Dunlop Street).
The Directors of the West of Scotland Electric Theatres, Limited, beg to announce that this Theatre IS NOW OPEN.

KINEMACOLOR
(the sole rights of which in the West of Scotland have been secured at great expense) will be shown, together with the Latest and Best Black and White Pictures.
KINEMACOLOR is revolutionising Kinematography.
KINEMACOLOR produces the World's events in their Natural Tints, Colours, and Movements.
KINEMACOLOR must not be confused with the crude hand-painted films now being shown in the various halls throughout the country.
The Theatre is magnificently fitted and upholstered throughout.
CONTINUOUS PERFORMANCE DAILY from 2 p.m. until 10.30 p.m.
ADMISSION—6d, 4d, and 2d.
Children Half-Price to 6d and 4d Seats.

(1910 advert, with kind permission from The Daily Record.)

NEW ELECTRIC THEATRE IN GLASGOW
To the number of cinematograph houses in Glasgow, another addition is the Argyle Electric Theatre which is situated in Argyle Street, near Dunlop Street. The establishment is under the management of the West of Scotland Electric Theatre Ltd who already run the Charring Cross Electric Theatre. There is an attractive exterior, designed by Mr George A. Boswell, Architect and the interior of the house, with its raked floor, is admirably suited for the comfort of patrons. Yesterday the theatre was open for private view, and the public continuous performances will begin today.
(The Scotsman 23 December 1910)

> *The Argyle Electric Theatre is run on the "continuous performance" principle and that "Kinemacolor" is a valuable asset. Manager Mr Fred Burnette is hustling in the right way.*
> (The Bioscope 5 January 1911)

> *Mr Fred Burnette is fairly making things "boom" at the splendidly equipped Argyle Electric Theatre. He has nothing to learn in the managerial art, and he puts his whole soul so thoroughly into his duties that success is bound to follow his efforts. He, as it were, not only deserves success but demands it as well.*
> (The Bioscope 30 March 1911)

The Argyle Electric Theatre underwent a rebuild in 1938 based on plans drawn by the same Architect, George A. Boswell, and was renamed the Argyle Picture House. However, the cinema closed in 1960 and was demolished in 1963 to make way for Argyle Street Station.

(Theatre de Luxe, image credit: Bruce Peter.)

Samuel and Emily had moved to a house at 5 Chisholm Street, around the corner from the Trongate, where Samuel made his first Glasgow appearance. Although Samuel was by now a cinema proprietor, he is listed on the 1911 Census as a photographer, and his sons, Victor and Herbert, were working for him. Victor was a photographer, and Herbert was an assistant. Emily D'Arc was living in the house under the guise of his Housekeeper. Samuel did not fulfil his three-year contract with the Argyle Electric, and it comes as no surprise that he was moving on to more significant, more ambitious projects.

The Theatre de Luxe Company of 164 Bath Street, Glasgow, was registered as a private company with a capital of £1000 in £1 shares. The first shareholders were listed as Mr Archibald McNiven, clerk, 31 Willow Bank Crescent and Mr Thomas H Courtenay, clerk, 393 Rutherglen Road.

Mr Fred Burnette has vacated the managerial capacity at The Argyle Electric Theatre, Glasgow to assume managing dictatorship of the new Theatre de Luxe in Sauchiehall Street. The occasion was marked by a presentation to Mr Burnette of a case of pipes, tobacco pouch and silver matchbox – handsome gifts given by the Argyle staff as a token of their esteem. Mr Burnette has proved himself one of the best Managers in the West of Scotland, and I and all his numerous friends wish him every success in his new sphere.

(The Bioscope 13 July 1911)

Theatre De Luxe

The Theatre de Luxe was opened on 16 November 1911 and received much positive coverage in the press at the time. The Bioscope complimented Mr F Rendell Burnette on a magnificent entertainment palace, where the comfort of its patrons was paramount. The article described the attention to detail of the seating arrangements, noting that the floor was set at a long sloping angle, allowing ladies to remain seated with their hats on for the full show. The latest 'illuminating screen' provided a very clear film presentation and would not tire the eyes had been installed. Hallways and corridors were spacious, allowing easy access to all parts of the cinema. Consideration had been given to the ample number of spacious lounges throughout the theatre where waiting cinemagoers could sit in luxury. The excellent opening performance was a balanced mix of gaiety and gravity to suit all tastes. The Theatre de Luxe promised to supply the most up-to-date films and provide a special children's performance each week. The article went on to explain some of Samuel's experience within the cinema industry, highlighting his various managerial roles in entertainment halls in both England and Scotland before opening a roller rink, which he later converted into the Argyle Electric Theatre. According to the Bioscope:

> *Mr Burnette is a gentleman who is the essence of courtesy and geniality, and there is no doubt that among the patrons of the new Theatre de Luxe, he will prove himself immensely popular.*
> (The Bioscope 23 November 1911)

A few months later, the Bioscope wrote a follow-up-article on the success of the Theatre de Luxe, highlighting the picturesque frontage with its coloured lights and its luxurious and superior interior. The article ended with high praise for Samuel:

> *Mr Burnette is full of new and novel ideas for working cinematograph houses, and the Theatre de Luxe is worthy of the high reputation of Mr Burnette.*
> (The Bioscope 25 January 1912)

In early February 1912, Samuel and his "wife" attended a dinner function back at his very first cinema: One hundred staff and associates of the Argyle Electric Theatre and Charing Cross Electric met for their first annual dinner, at which Samuel gave an appreciative speech.

Sometime between 1911 and 1912, Samuel and Frederick parted ways, each pursuing their own individual enterprises. While Frederick Stewart went to Belfast to open his own cinema, Samuel stayed in Glasgow and formed a new company. The De Luxe Picture House Ltd was formed with £7500 in £1 shares to acquire The Theatre De Luxe Company. (Both owned by Samuel) The first directors were Robert Smith, hotel proprietor; A. McCardle; Frederick Rendell Burnette, cinema proprietor; and A.V. Gardner, architect.

Such was the success of the de Luxe picture house that it was deemed too small an enterprise. In October 1912, Samuel applied to the Dean of Guild for permission to make extensive alterations to the building in order to accommodate a much larger audience. The Theatre de Luxe underwent an extension and refurbishment less than two years after its original opening. Money was spent upgrading the equipment to keep up to date with the new technology of the time. When the cinema reopened, the operating room had two machines, a Pathe and a Silent Empire. According to The Bioscope newspaper, those who had visited the old hall would not recognise the upgraded theatre. A suite of sumptuous tea rooms and retiring rooms now occupied the site of the old theatre. A new auditorium, built at street level, was accessed through a splendid lounge furnished with comfortable sofas, and the whole interior was decorated in the style of Louis XIV, in a cream and gold colour palette, creating an illusion of grandeur. The newly installed ventilation system provided an agreeable atmosphere throughout the whole theatre, and the extra exits allowed the hall to be emptied quickly and easily. The Bioscope included special praise for the architect:

In the roof a striking feature is a trio of cupolas of stained glass, and altogether Mr A.V. Gardner, the architect responsible for the whole scheme, is to be highly commended for the beauty of the completed conception, and also for the practical manner in which he has realised the possibilities of the building.
(The Bioscope 16 January 1913)

When Samuel resigned from his position as manager of the de Luxe in September 1913, the staff presented him with a gold-mounted umbrella.

The Theatre de Luxe continued its popularity with cinema-goers, earning a reputation as one of the best picture houses in Glasgow. The Kinematograph publication claimed that no other theatre in the city provided a better-selected or more balanced programme of films, with the house orchestra being an attraction in itself. The Theatre de Luxe remained in business until 1930 when it was forced to close due to competition from later, much larger cinema venues.
1912 was to prove one of the busiest for Samuel, with many business projects on the go at the same time. The Theatre de Luxe on Sauchiehall Street was an instant success with audiences, thanks to the latest technology and its high standard of luxury, and so Samuel was free to turn his attention to a new cinema. But this time, not just one new cinema but four.

PARTICK PICTURE HOUSE

(Partick Picture House, image credit: Chris Doak.)

The first of the four new cinemas was another collaboration with the architect A.V. Gardner in Partick. A private company was formed in February 1912, with a capital of £3500, in connection with the Partick Picture House. Mr R Davidson, Partick and Mr J McMahon, Rutherglen, were the subscribers. The Partick Picture House was opened on 4th November 1912. The cinema, built to accommodate 900 patrons, was located on Orchard Street, in the centre of a densely populated area. The sandstone building was designed as an old Scottish baronial castle, with two imposing towers at the entrance, which housed the ticket kiosks. The interior was luxurious and spacious, with the balcony being one of the deepest and highest in Glasgow. The cinema boasted two Pathe machines, the latest improved screen, and an orchestra of four musicians. According to the Bioscope newspaper, " A diffused light is maintained throughout the auditorium – 'a dim, religious light – to be correct.'

Samuel decided to make this a real family business by employing his son Bertie as an apprentice projectionist, hopeful that he would learn the trade and become part of Samuel's expanding empire. As with Samuel's first cinemas, the Partick Picture House was a huge success with locals and was a well-attended cinema that went from strength to strength. As was the custom in the west of Scotland, the cinema celebrated its birthday with a dinner dance the following November. Although Samuel was not present at the occasion, the chairman made a speech praising both Samuel and George Taylor for their management skills. By January 1914, Samuel had resigned from his post as managing director of the picture house and George Taylor was appointed sole manager. Partick Picture House underwent a rebuild from 1919 to 1921 and from 1930 to 1931, with A.V Gardner acting as architect on each occasion. In February 1957, a fire broke out and damaged the roof, balcony and stalls. Occupants in nearby tenements were evacuated as flames leapt through the roof, shattering the asbestos in a series of explosions. Firemen saved the vestibule and prevented the fire from spreading to the surrounding properties. The cinema was eventually demolished in 1962.

THEATRE DE LUXE ROTHESAY

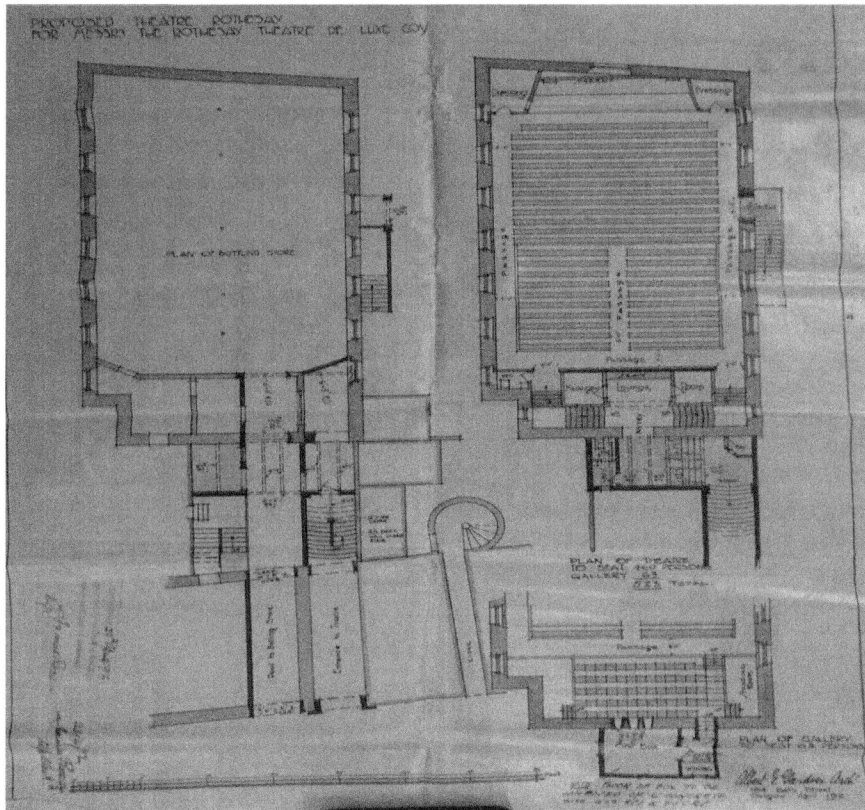

(Theatre de Luxe Rothesay, image credit: Live Argyll.)

While Samuel was busy throughout the year preparing for the opening of the Picture House in Partick, he had also been busy juggling the opening of two other cinemas simultaneously. One was the Star Palace in Maryhill, Glasgow, and the other was the Theatre de Luxe in Rothesay. The Rothesay Theatre De Luxe Limited was re-registered in Edinburgh on 25th April 1912 with a capital of £1200 in £1 shares.

The first directors were F.R Burnette, J. Cunningham, J. Lyle, D McKinnon, M. O'Connor and R. Smith. The directors were all local Rothesay businessmen who were known to Samuel. Martin O'Connor owned a wine and spirit merchants at Gallowgate, their slogan being, "Family orders punctually attended to." Both John Cunningham and Duncan McKinnon owned well-established aerated water companies in the town. John Lyle was the owner of the Lorne Hotel, which sat on the waterfront directly opposite the quayside. Robert Smith had been a baker in Glasgow, but by the time Samuel made his acquaintance, he was the owner of the Bute Arms Hotel on Guilford Square, opposite the pier.

The architect for the project was A. V. Gardner, who was tasked with converting a bottling store into a cinema. The finished picture theatre had a 30 feet wide proscenium and had a British Thomson Houston sound system. Samuel appointed Allan McFadyen as the cinema's resident manager.

> Early in June, it is expected that the new Rothesay Picture Palace, in Montague Street, will be opened, and during the summer season three shows will be given daily. Seating accommodation of the most up to date kind will be provided for and audience of 700 and with Mr F.R. Burnette as the managing director, it may be assumed that only the brightest and best programmes will be submitted. I predict for Mr Burnette's new hall a most emphatic success.
> (The Bioscope 18 April 1912.)

This article has three errors: The Theatre de Luxe was situated on Store Lane, not Montague Street. Samuel's Rothesay cinema was called the Theatre de Luxe, not Rothesay Picture Palace, and the architect's plans show a seating capacity for 523, not 700.

The local newspaper, The Buteman, carried several reports and updates in the run-up to the grand opening of the De Luxe. In one article, Samuel was described as "A gentleman who is the essence of geniality and courtesy."

Samuel aimed to provide Rothesay cinemagoers with the most recent films, including weekly children's matinee shows. He placed an advert in The Buteman on 30th August 1912, announcing the motto: "We aim to amuse, entertain and educate." He then challenged the locals to "See every picture theatre in Rothesay, then see ours. We stand by your verdict."

The actual opening date for the cinema has proved to be rather elusive. The Early Cinema in Scotland research project claims it was July 1912, although there is no evidence source, while both the Kinematograph Weekly and The Bioscope state August 1912. The Theatre de Luxe was an instant hit with both the local population of Rothesay and visiting holidaymakers. The entrance was an eye-catching domed tower, which led to a wide staircase opening into the auditorium and gallery. The entire theatre had been fitted out with tip-up chairs to seat 550 people. Samuel spared no expense when it came to the latest technology, employing engineers from Glasgow to install the screen, gas engine and dynamo film projector. On the opening night, there were two shows. Invited guests, including members of the press, attended a private showing followed by a reception. This was followed by the first public performance, with every seat filled. The de Luxe ran a programme of two showings every evening in addition to Saturday matinees.

Samuel opened the cinema in Rothesay in time to make the most of summer holidaymakers. As with his previous cinemas, the Theatre de Luxe, Rothesay, was a success. Just a year after opening, Samuel invested more money and installed the latest British Thomson Huston projector.

In March 1913, Samuel delighted the people of Rothesay by securing Capellani's French film Les Miserables. At this time, to be commercially viable, a film lasted approximately 30 minutes because filmmakers assumed that audiences wouldn't sit through a film any longer than that. Condensing Victor Hugo's epic tale into 30 minutes was an impossible task, so Capellani came up with the idea of creating a series four films, each lasting 40 minutes. The film was released in France in January 1913 over four consecutive weeks, and so began the serial film genre. This innovative and unique achievement changed the course of cinema history. All modern blockbusters are the result of Albert Capellani's daring idea. The twelve-reel film ran for a total of 160 minutes and had a massive impact on the Rothesay audiences. Every show was sold out, and extra tramway cars were put on each evening to transport people from the Port Bannatyne area. As reported in the bioscope, "Rothesay people like good pictures and the de Luxe sees that they get them."

Samuel must have had some friends in high places if he was able to arrange extra tram cars to be provided for people going to the pictures for a night out! Samuel had a love of new technology and all things electrical and mechanical. Because of one newspaper article, it could also be argued that he had an interest in football. However, it is more likely that Samuel was employing his business and marketing skills, making valuable contacts that he knew would generate good press coverage:

> At the new theatre de Luxe in Rothesay, Mr Burnette is displaying his customary enterprise, and as an instance in point, it may be mentioned that a recent sojourn of the Glasgow rangers football club to this popular watering place found a hearty invitation being extended to the members of the team and officials to visit the entertainment. I need hardly say that the hospitality on the part of Mr Burnette was greatly appreciated by the "light blues," and the famous footballers certainly spent a most enjoyable time at his up-to-date cinema house. This new theatre which continues to be under the management of me Allan McFadyen, is still meeting with the greatest possible success.
> (The Bioscope 6th February 1913)

(Theatre de Luxe Rothesay, image credit: Ian Armstrong.)

Just two years after opening, Samuel appointed a new manager for his De Luxe Cinema. Fred W Nettleton had been assistant manager in the De Luxe before his promotion. He had begun his career as a concert artiste, performing in shows across Germany and Austria. He had also been part of Catlin's Royal Pierrot Troupe before branching out on his own as a comedian, actor, and singer. During the war years, he did his bit working in one of the Greenock shipyards while his wife took on the role of manager at the cinema. He became highly regarded and sought after in the cinema world and later became manager of various establishments in Edinburgh, Dundee and the Glasgow area.

(Street sign for Rothesay de Luxe, image credit: Bute Museum.)

Samuel created his own bit of wartime history. In 1914, just after the outbreak of war, he commissioned a film showing the Bute Territorials departing for war on Clyde Steamers, which was screened in his Rothesay picture house. In 1923, Samuel bought the Rothesay de Luxe outright from the original company of which he had been a founding member and first managing director. He wasted no time in undertaking a refurbishment of both the interior and exterior of the building, including an upgrade to the lighting effects for the screen. He undoubtably had big plans for taking his new business forward. Unfortunately, one year later, Samuel was in difficulty, and the cinema went into liquidation.

> *The Rothesay theatre de Luxe limited (in voluntary liquidation)*
> *Notice is hereby given,, in pursuance of section 195 of the companies (consolidation) act 1908 that a general meeting of the members of the above named company will be held within the Norman Stewart institute, Rothesay on Wednesday 14th January 1925, at 5 o' clock afternoon, for the purpose of having the accounts laid before them, showing the manner in which the winding up has been conducted and the property of the company disposed of; of hearing any explanation that may be given by the liquidator; and of fixing the liquidator's remuneration; and also to determine, by extra ordinary resolution, the manner in which the books, accounts and documents of the company and liquidator shall be disposed of.*
> *Dated this 9th day of December 1924.*
> *Wm Watson, liquidator.*

This must have been a significant financial nightmare for Samuel. However, not one to give up, he found a way to settle his business debts without having to sell the cinema. In 1924, he was listed as the proprietor, and the cinema was undergoing improvements. According to Scottish Valuation Rolls, the improvements continued until 1940, when the cinema closed during the war years. Samuel sold it to Palace Theatre Ltd, and then it became a lemonade factory and, later, a joint premises for a blacksmith and a bookmaker. The cinema was devastated by a fire and eventually demolished, but there are conflicting reports as to exactly when this happened.

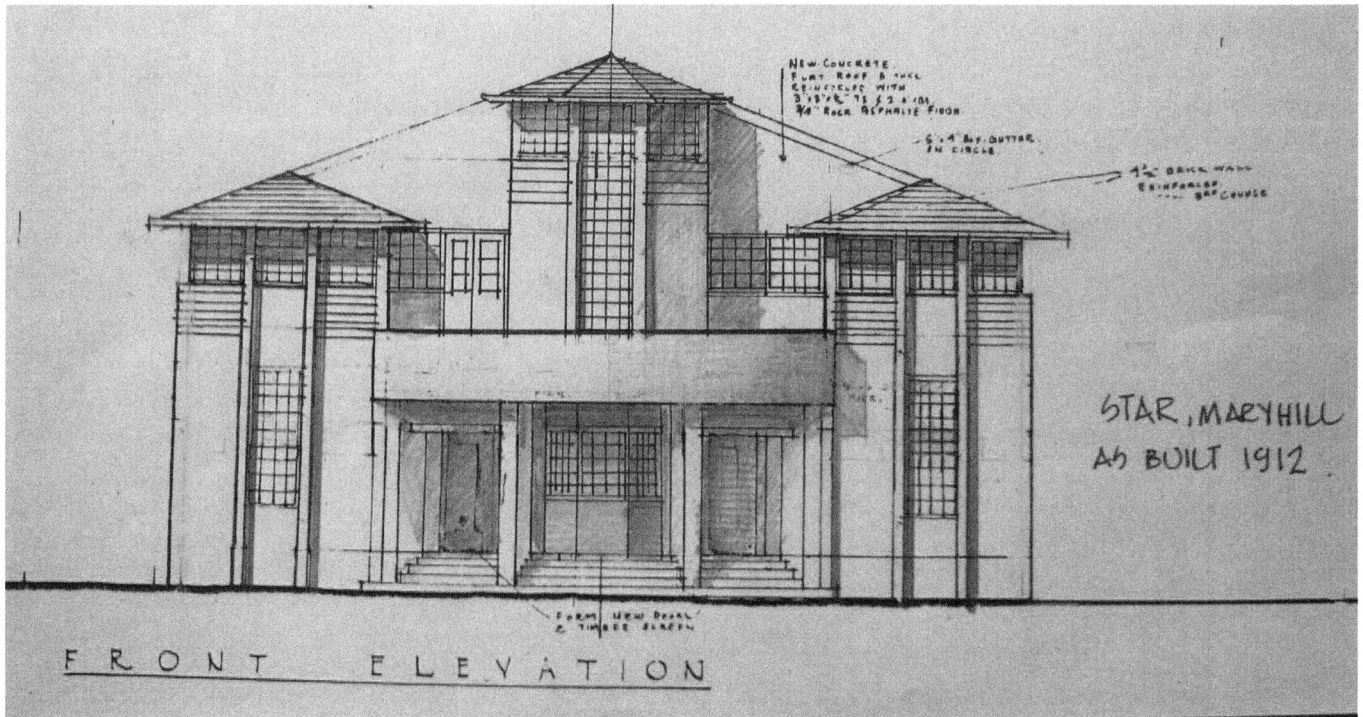

(Maryhill Star Palace, image credit: Chris Doak.)

With two cinemas opened in 1912, Samuel was about to open his third of the year. On 28th May 1912, the Maryhill Star Palace Ltd was registered in Edinburgh with a capital of £3000 in £1 shares. The first directors, with 100 shares each, were Mr R. Davidson, J Levi, and J. McMahon. Again, Samuel had convinced local businessmen and acquaintances to invest in his cinema. Robert Davidson was a salesman with interests in Glasgow billiard halls, and John McMahon and Jacob Levi were already shareholders and directors in Samuel's other cinemas. Not to be confused with other Glasgow cinemas of the time with "Star" in their name, the Maryhill Star Palace was located at 1046 Maryhill Road. A.V. Gardner designed it to seat 900, almost twice the size of Samuel's cinema in Rothesay.

> *Mr Fred R. Burnette is at present an extremely busy man and he now has various enterprises to which he is giving his personal attention. At the moment his energies are largely concentrated upon the new theatre de Luxe in Rothesay – which will be open for the benefit of seaside visitors and local residents a month hence – and the new Partick picture house and both of these halls are on the well-known "Burnette" lines. Mr Burnette's latest venture is a new hall in Maryhill, which will be called the star palace, and in this popular district of Glasgow it is bound to meet with the success which attends all his ventures. Undoubtably Mr Burnette is one of the leaders of the picture palace industry in the west of Scotland and I wish him ever continuing success.*
> (The Bioscope 6th June 1912)

High praise indeed for Samuel to be considered a "leader" of the industry on the west coast of Scotland. Samuel had come a long way from performing parlour tricks in schoolrooms and a life on the road with a travelling waxwork show.

Samuel was placing the Maryhill Star in experienced hands. William Howgate had been the manager of the Glasgow Grand Theatre and worked for Moss Empire Ltd for four years as deputy manager of the Glasgow Empire. He then went into partnership with Alex Keith at the Zoo Hippodrome, Glasgow, where he presented picture and variety programmes with great success. Mr Howgate relied on a tried and tested mixture of cinema and live performances for the Maryhill Star. I can't help but think the idea of live variety would have appealed to Samuel.

> *On paying his initial visit to the new star palace at Maryhill, "scotty" was delighted to find that every seat was occupied, and he was greatly impressed with the cosy and comfortable appearance of the hall. The proprietors are to be heartily congratulated on their appointment of Mr William Howgate as general manager, and no wiser choice could have been made than this gentleman as far as guiding the destinies of the "star" is concerned. the "star" is running an excellent programme, combining the latest of pictures and the best of variety turns and as the hall accommodates such a large audience as 1,200 people – it will at once be seen that it is planned on big lines. The scheme of decoration is carried out principally in grey toned colours, and the finished effect is certainly very pretty pleasing. The designer of the hall was Mr Gardner, the well-known local architect and he is to be complimented on his conception both of the interior and exterior.*
> (The Bioscope 30th January 1913)

This article contradicts the information from the previous *Bioscope* article regarding the seating capacity, so perhaps Gardner's plans were altered before the build began. Maryhill Star Palace underwent a rebuild and enlargement in 1930 to seat 1,799 people, with A.V. Gardner as the architect again. It was closed in 1966 and later became a car salesroom before being demolished in 1978.

CAMPBELTOWN PICTURE HOUSE

(Campbeltown Picture House, image credit: Richard Stenlake Collection.)

The final cinema in 1912 to occupy Samuel's attention was the new Picture House in Campbeltown. The Picture House Campbeltown Limited, a private company, was registered in Edinburgh on 16 August 1912 with a capital of £2500 in £1 shares. The first directors were Archibald Dunlop Armour, plumber, Longrow, Campbeltown; S. Armour, Ironmonger, Longrow, Campbeltown; James Smith, hotel keeper, Ugadale Arms Hotel, Machrihanish; Fred. Rendell Burnette, managing director, Theatre de Luxe, Glasgow. This company was registered on the same day as the De Luxe Picture House Ltd Company (Glasgow), which shows how many plates in the air Samuel was spinning in 1912.

The Directors of the Picture House were some of Campbeltown's most influential and well-connected businessmen. James Smith was the son of Robert Smith, a director of Samuel's Rothesay cinema. James Smith was the head clerk of the Central Hotel in Glasgow for a time before arriving in Kintyre. Captain Hector Macneal, the Laird of Ugadale, had completely upgraded and renovated the hotel, introducing electric lights throughout. The hotel now had sixty bedrooms, a large drawing room, six parlours, two billiard rooms, a smoke room, a dining room and five bathrooms. In 1902, James Smith became the hotel's proprietor when Captain Macneal advertised the hotel for let with immediate entry. James was very forward-thinking in attracting clients to his hotel by combining excursions and entertainment as part of the holiday experience. He was also very clever in marketing the hotel, placing adverts in newspapers north and south of the border. The hotel was advertised as a golfing paradise on the shores of the Atlantic, a health resort, an escape from the worries of modern life. Every comfort and convenience were offered, including an American bar and hot and cold water in every room. James even produced an illustrated booklet, which was available to view before booking. James made a huge impact, and the business was so successful that he later became the managing director of the Ugadale.

Apart from sharing the same surname and place of birth, Samuel Armour and Archibald Dunlop Armour were not related. Born in Campbeltown, the son of a maltman, Samuel Armour began his working life as a travelling metal salesman before returning to Campbeltown to start his own Ironmongers business on Longrow. In 1906, he became one of the founding members and directors of Campbeltown Bowling Club. While still running his Ironmongers, he became the only independent Stockbroker in the town.

Archibald Dunlop Armour was born into a family of coppersmiths, tinsmiths, gasfitters and plumbers who ran their business for many generations on Longrow in Campbeltown. They were an incredibly wealthy family, with much of their money having come from Archibald's grandfather, Robert Armour. Robert Armour used his plumbing business as a front for his illegal, illicit, still-making enterprise, supplying much of Kintyre, the islands, and beyond with whisky stills. Archibald Dunlop Armour took on the family business and continued its success for many years, the financial rewards allowing him to become a wealthy property owner. In addition, he was an active member in public life within the town: he was a Librarian for Longrow Church, a debating member of the Literary Institute, a volunteer with the Argyll Rifles, chairman of the board of the Campbeltown and Glasgow Steam Packet Joint Stock Company, Convener of the new Grammar School, President of Kintyre Agricultural Society, a founding member of Campbeltown Bowling Club, a Justice of the Peace and an early member of Kintyre Antiquarian Society. Although he had a passion for the past, he was considered by all who knew him to be a very forward-thinking man and is credited with being instrumental in the inception of the Campbeltown Picture House.

We understand that a local syndicate has been formed to erect and carry on a picture palace in Campbeltown, the site of which is in hall street, near royal avenue mansions. It is stated the managing director to be appointed is in close touch with the most up to date picture houses in Glasgow. The plans are now being prepared, and we understand accommodation will be arranged for about 700 persons and the theatre will be modern in every respect.
(The Argyllshire herald 22 June 1912)

(Shares ledger, image credit: Campbeltown Community Business Ltd.)

In 1912, the syndicate leased a plot of land located on Hall Street on the shore of Campbeltown Loch. The land belonged to Mrs Jeanie McQueen, the widow of Archibald McQueen, a retired shipbuilder and an ex-Bailie of Campbeltown. The plot of land was later bought by the syndicate in 1921. F. R. Burnette was appointed as managing director of the Picture House. Many local Campbeltown businessmen and local women bought shares in the company, including whisky distillers, hotel keepers, plumbers, shopkeepers, bankers, builders and even a minister's daughter. F.R. Burnette bought 150 of the original shares in 1912 and convinced William D'Arc, brother of Emily D'Arc, to buy 50 shares.

It will come as no surprise that the architect was A.V Gardner. He designed the Picture House in the Glasgow Art Nouveau style, with oeil de boeuf windows and a deep recessed balcony under a superstructure of concentric oval forms. The original hand-drawn detailed plans, coloured and signed by A. V. Gardner. The detailed plans show the front and side elevations, cross-sections and internal layouts of the ground floor, gallery and cine box. The account ledger shows that A. V. Gardner was paid three amounts of cash, £50, £20 and £30 between 1912 and 1914.

The original shares ledger and accounts ledger of the cinema still survive and give incredible insight to the people involved in making the Picture House become a reality in less than a year. Much of the construction work was carried out by local tradespeople, with Glasgow contractors responsible for the surveying, the steelworks and the roof for the cinema. The building account page of the accounts book shows dated payments to the companies involved in the actual building of the cinema.

Neil McArthur was an experienced local builder who had the contract for the masonry work on the cinema. He was paid a total of £539, 13s, 10d. for his work. He was also an original shareholder who bought 36 shares. Dugald McSporran, a local joiner, was paid six cash amounts between 1912 and 1914 for his work totalling £449, 2s, 2d. Robert Armour, a local plumber, and half-brother of Archibald Dunlop Armour, was paid £90 for his work. An original shareholder, Robert bought 50 shares in 1912. James Hall, a local carpenter, was paid £88 1s for his work, and N. McPherson, son of a local family business of slaters and plasterers, was paid £98 1s.

> *While speaking of Mr Burnette, I may mention that this enterprising gentleman has arranged to "invade" Campbeltown. at the moment an up-to-date picture theatre is in the course of erection in this watering place, and it is expected to be ready in good time for the summer season. The architect is Mr Albert V. Gardner – who by the way, is also responsible for the plans for a new picture theatre which is to be erected in the watering place of Dunoon.*
> (The Bioscope 6 March 1913)

In the week leading up to the opening of the Picture House, the local newspaper carried the following report:

OPENING OF NEW PICTURE HOUSE
The new picture house in Hall Street, the first venture of its kind in town, will be open on Monday first. the appointments of the house are first class, and compare favourably with the best picture theatres in the west of Scotland. patrons will have the privilege of obtaining comfort such as has never before been found at entertainments of any kind in this town. The management too, aiming are aiming at a high-class entertainment, and the programme for the opening week should at once ensure the popularity of the venture. there will be two houses nightly, and the price of admission range from 6d to 1s.
(The Campbeltown courier 24 May 1913)

(Advert for Campbeltown Picture House, image credit: Campbeltown Courier.)

The Argyllshire Herald went into more detail:

The Campbeltown picture house
opens next week
While there has been some delay in the completion of the local picture house, the finishing touches
are now being put on, and it is expected that this place of entertainment will be formally opened on
Monday, when the directors have invited a large company to be present at the inauguration.
Naturally one prefers to see the progress of home industries and home schemes, and the picture
house is really a home scheme, for the directors are resident here, and the shareholders are, for the
most part, also of Campbeltown. We have seen how successful these entertainments may be in the
town, and there is every reason to hope that the present venture will be successful. During the past
week the workmen engaged in the completion of the picture house have been busy late and early,
and the frequent display of lights has intimated to the public that the opening of Campbeltown's own
place of entertainment is near at hand.
We had opportunity to inspect the picture house this week, and what we saw on that occasion
impressed us very much. the auditorium is thoroughly business like, well seated with comfortable tip
up seats, while the seating in the gallery is of quite a luxurious character. The electric light
installation is very complete and the dynamo is driven by a 16 h.p. gas engine of improved type. In
the front of the building above the gallery is the operator's chamber, and there we were privileged to
see the cinematograph really at work, with its light of 12,000 candle power.The arrangements for
safety are very complete, and the machine, being of the latest type, includes every improvement
which makes for the safety of the operator, and the audience generally. The whole building seems to
be very compact and complete in detail. for instance, there are telephones in various parts, so that
communication is maintained between the various points, while the lighting is controlled from the
operator's chamber.
The colour scheme is up to date, and is decidedly attractive, but as yet there is considerable painting
and touch up to be done.
On the whole, however, the building is well adapted for its purpose, and we believe that when it is in
proper working order, it will be considerably sought after as a place of entertainment.
(The Argyllshire herald 24 May 1913)

The Campbeltown Picture House was opened on Monday, 26 May 1913. The management put on a special programme of films for invited guests and shareholders, and afternoon tea was provided. George Finlay Roger was the first manager of the Picture House. He was a successful photographer who owned several studios before and during his Picture House employment. At the time of his appointment, his studio was a few doors along from the cinema.

The opening of the Picture House was given much coverage in local newspapers. One article from the Campbeltown Courier concentrated on Samuel, the new Managing Director. However, some of the information in the article is somewhat suspect as it is without evidence:

> *The managing director: There is no better-known personage in the picture house world than the subject of the above photograph. Mr Burnette is a pioneer of the business. Born in England, he wisely saw the future that was in store for the moving pictures, and as America was far ahead of this country in that business, he went over there to get a complete knowledge at first hand, and that knowledge has been invaluable to him. He acquired a connection with all the leading American firms, and today the public of this country know the benefit of his thorough grasp of all the details of the wants of a picture house. His connection is large. Among some of the popular theatres he controls are the Theatre de Luxe, Partick Picture House, Rothesay de Luxe, Campbeltown, Inverness and a large northern circuit. With this connection he is able to obtain the latest photo plays etc, exclusively for his places of entertainment.*
>
> *Mr Burnette has had many adventures in the course of his travels. One of his recent exploits was earlier this year. He had an appointment in Campbeltown in connection with his new picture house there and made up his mind to go there by the road in his motor. But the great landslide at the "rest and be thankful" almost upset this arrangement, for when he arrived there the road was completely blocked. To turn back meant a detour of nearly forty miles. doing so, he could not have got to his destination in time for his appointment so he drove right over the debris along the mountainside. His car at times was perilously near toppling over the broken hillside, and at parts of the way he was compelled to get the assistance of the road workers to clear the huge boulders from the path. After a thrilling journey he got to his destination, his little "ford" being none the worse. he has travelled in this car throughout Scotland and England over 30,000 miles, and has not yet missed an appointment.*
>
> (Campbeltown Courier 31 may 1913)

I think that this article highlights how determined a character Samuel was. He could have taken the detour, or he could have rescheduled the meeting. He could even have travelled by steamboat to reach Campbeltown. He wasn't without options, but his exploits give an idea of his sense of adventure or possibly his dogged recklessness. Samuel had a love of motor cars, and the following year, Samuel wrote off his car when he overturned it into a ditch. Fortunately, Samuel and his passengers escaped with only a severe shaking.

The main aim of this article is to illustrate Samuel's high level of skill and knowledge of the cinema industry, underlining the vast experience of his time spent in the business. However, no evidence or documentation supports the claim that Samuel spent time in America to learn his trade. From 1906 until 1909, he was concerned with establishing his mechanical show, roller rink and photography business. After that, he entered the world of cinema, and opening one cinema after another would have left no time for travel to the U.S.A. I can't see when he would have had the time to visit America to learn new technology skills – and his finances would not have afforded such a trip. He didn't start to make his money until after opening his first picture house, and after that, he was on a whirlwind of activity, opening his subsequent cinemas. Samuel's time in Glasgow would have given him access to the latest American technology and films, and this is probably where the "American" connection myth was born. At that time, Glasgow had been dubbed "Cinema City" and, in its heyday, would eventually have more than 170 cinemas. It is also possible that Samuel was using some poetic licence regarding his career for the interview article.

The article also claims that Samuel had cinemas in Inverness and a large Northern Circuit, but there is only one short mention of Inverness in an article dated 1913:

In the course of an interesting conversation with Mr Fred Rendell Burnette, he informed me that he had tendered his resignation as manager with the Theatre de Luxe Sauchiehall Street Glasgow. Mr Burnette, as everyone in the business knows, acts as managing director of several picture house companies in Scotland and is one of the pioneers of kinematography in this country. A born showman, full of hustle and a lover of hard work, Mr Burnette finds life in Glasgow – especially at such a quiet and well-ordered theatre as the de Luxe, rather slow after the work of organising and building up the business of the house. Having been requested to take over the formation and management of several new suburban concerns Mr Burnette – seeing in such congenial work plenty of hustle and excitement – has decided to devote his whole time and ability making the new concerns as successful as the de Luxe. The latter theatre has been phenomenally successful and Mr Burnette had to build a new theatre beside the old with three times the capacity of the original hall. among his new charges are theatres at Inverness and Dumbarton, at present in course of formation and several others under construction.
(Kinematograph and Lantern weekly 11 September 1913)

Those involved in the moving picture entertainment business would have been well-known to each other within Scotland. It is quite conceivable that investors, directors and other interested parties would have visited cinemas around Scotland to check out the competition. Therefore, it is likely that Samuel was well acquainted with cinema owners in Inverness. He possibly had every intention of opening a new picture house there, but there is no further evidence or mention of his connection with such a cinema after the 1913 article. As for the Dumbarton cinemas, there is no connection there either. It is possible that he had shares in other cinema companies or perhaps acted in some advisory role. He did talk a good talk.

The Campbeltown Picture House was a huge hit with locals and visitors alike, and a follow-up report appeared in the local press after the grand opening:

It is a rare compliment to the fare at the new picture house that the attendance for the second week should have been much better than they were in the opening week. The cult of the picture theatre is obviously growing on local folks, and everybody appears to be delighted with the show. The children's Saturday matinee proved a popular arrangement last week, and the Saturday evening house was packed. A fascinating programme has been arranged for next week, and what is yet to run of this week's is worth seeing.
(The Campbeltown Courier 7 June 1913)

Just a few months after the Campbeltown opening, Samuel resigned from his position with the Glasgow de Luxe cinema to concentrate on his other business interests.

Mr F. R. Burnette has resigned his position as the managing director of the Theatre de Luxe, Sauchiehall Street, Glasgow. This enterprising gentleman is, at the moment, associated with three of the most successful picture halls on Scottish soil – namely, at Rothesay, at Partick and at Campbeltown – and he keeps himself, as is his wont, fully abreast of every development in the cinematography industry. Mr Burnette is capably supported by his various managers, namely, Mr Allan McFadyen at the Rothesay de Luxe, Mr George Taylor at the Partick Picture House and by Mr George Rodgers at the Campbeltown Picture House.
(The Bioscope 23 October 1913)

CAMPBELTOWN INVADED

BY

F. R. BURNETTE, Managing Director,

AND HIS

STAFF AND CINE. OPERATOR

to take a Picture at the Pierhead of the

ARGYLL and SUTHERLAND HIGHLANDERS

on their arrival on SATURDAY & SUNDAY AFTERNOONS by the Steamers Kylemore and Queen Alexandra.

After the Invasion

you will be able to see yourself take DEFEAT WITH A HAPPY SMILE at the PICTURE HOUSE on TUESDAY EVENING and during the week.

(Advert 1914, image credit: Campbeltown Courier.)

On the 17th and 18th of July 1914, the 6th, 7th, and 9th battalions of the Argyll and Sutherland Highlanders arrived by steamer at Campbeltown Quay, ready to attend their annual training camp at Machrihanish. The training schedules for each battalion had been published in national newspapers in March, and Samuel took advantage of this information to create a publicity stunt for the Campbeltown cinema. He commissioned a Gaumont film to show his journey from the Argyll Motor Works in Alexandria to Campbeltown Quay in a large, open Argyll motor car. On arrival at the quayside, the film would capture the disembarking battalions and their parade through the town as they marched off to their training ground at Clochkeil, Machrihanish. The three battalions, along with two half companies from Stirling and Grangemouth, numbered more than 2,500 men.

Samuel placed an announcement in newspapers, inviting local people to come to the quayside and be part of the film. The film was shown to Campbeltown audiences throughout the following week and was later shown in the Rothesay De Luxe cinema.

The significance and importance of this film were only realised after it had aired in both cinemas. On the 31st of August, the training exercise was complete, and the battalions left Campbeltown. Four days later, Britain was at war with Germany, and the young soldiers in Samuel's film would soon see active service in France.

Sadly, the film was damaged, and only a small portion of it survives. However, it is held by the National Library of Scotland as part of their moving image archive and can be viewed online. A few short appearances of Samuel in his film have also survived.

CHAPTER FIFTEEN

FINGERS IN LOTS OF PIES

(Samuel in his regalia, image credit: Ian Armstrong.)

From 1912 until the end of 1913, Samuel's business interests had been very much focused on opening his cinemas. After each cinema opening, Samuel would have been very involved in the day-to-day running to ensure continued success and to protect his financial investments. Samuel and Emily were still very much together. Shortly after the dust had settled on all the grand picture house openings, they moved from 5 Chisholm Street at the Trongate and bought a 19th-century terraced house at 22 Hamilton Drive in Glasgow. At some point during those Glasgow years, Samuel became a Royal Arch Freemason.

Although settled into life in Glasgow, Samuel had his photography studios in Rothesay to manage, so he would have been back on the road, just like his early days, taking care of business. Not content to have studios in Glasgow and Rothesay, in 1914, Samuel opened a photography showroom and studio in Stranraer, which he ran for at least ten years. This new studio would have meant yet more travelling for Samuel, but with his love of cars and driving, I am sure this would have been an enjoyable experience rather than a chore.

Mr Burnette, in photography as well as kinematography, believes in giving his patrons the best of good value, and that is possibly why he has been so supremely successful in both business operations. Mr. Burnette is a man of push and go.
(Kinematograph Weekly 17 January 1918)

It would be interesting, however, to have known what Emily thought of Samuel's passion for business, never content to settle with what he had built up so far, always looking for the next new adventure. In 1914, Samuel decided to buy property in Rothesay and become a landlord. One property was a large four-storey villa on Ardbeg Road. Samuel let the property out to eight tenants, earning him an annual rental income of £226 in the first year. The other property was much smaller, a tenement building in East Princes Street, several doors along from one of his studios. The rental income for the first year was £80. This is equivalent to a total annual income of over £33,000 today.

The 1914 Electoral Rolls show Samuel as an electrical engineer, operating his business out of an office above the Argyle Electric Theatre at 55 Argyle Street, the location of one of his photography studios. With so many business interests located in the centre of Glasgow, it made sense for Samuel to have accommodation within the city centre, so he rented a flat a few doors along from the Theatre de Luxe at 425 Sauchiehall Street, and at the same time, rented a garage in Bath Lane, Glasgow. There is no evidence to say whether the garage was another business venture or for private use – probably the latter because it made sense for him to have easy access to his motor car while working in the city.

Although unmarried, Samuel and Emily D'Arc were now living openly as man and wife. The British Journal of Photography in 1918 lists Mr Frederick Rendell Burnette at 108 Renfield Street, Glasgow, and the Electoral Rolls of 1918 show Mr Fred Rendell Burnette and Mrs Emily Burnette living at the same address. The Post Office Directory of 1919 listed Samuel's studios at 55 and 186 Argyle Street, the office at 108 Renfield Street and his home at 22 Hamilton Drive. All subsequent Electoral Rolls list Samuel and Emily as a married couple.

In 1920, Samuel opened another shop at 8 Kelvinside Avenue, Glasgow. There is no further clue as to the type of shop, but it was possibly another studio. Back in Rothesay, Samuel rented street advertising spaces at 9 Watergate, presumably for his Theatre de Luxe, as Watergate is adjacent to the cinema's location.

Sometime between 1920 and 1925, Samuel decided to branch out and begin a new business. The Electoral Rolls of 1925 and 1926 show Mr Frederick R Burnette and Mrs Emily Burnette at 128 Hope Street, Glasgow. Like Renfield Street, this property had living accommodation within the building. Would Samuel have been aware of the gravitas and cultural history of this address? Sisters Margaret and Frances MacDonald registered at the Glasgow School of Art in 1890. While studying at the school, the sisters met Charles Rennie Mackintosh and his friend Herbert McNair. The sisters left the school in 1894, and by 1895, they had set up their city art studio at 128 Hope Street. The sisters often collaborated with Charles Rennie Mackintosh and Herbert McNair, earning themselves the title "The Glasgow Four." Frances married Herbert McNair in 1899, and Margaret married Charles Rennie Mackintosh in 1900. However, unlike the Glasgow Four, Samuel wasn't setting up an art studio.

(Image credit: Ian Armstrong.)

128 Hope Street became the head office of his music business. He launched The Perfecto Gramophone Company, with a smaller branch at Dean Hood Place in Rothesay. Samuel became the Scottish agent for The Royal, Imperial and Academy Gramophones. Eventually, he was also the agent for Colombia Records, Zonophone Records and Regal Records. As well as gramophones, his shop sold musical instruments and accessories. He had certainly moved on from his days travelling around playing his cumbersome Concertophone! Glasgow Post Office Directories of 1925 also show F.R. Burnette at another address, 128 West George Lane, Glasgow, but unfortunately, there is no description of the business.

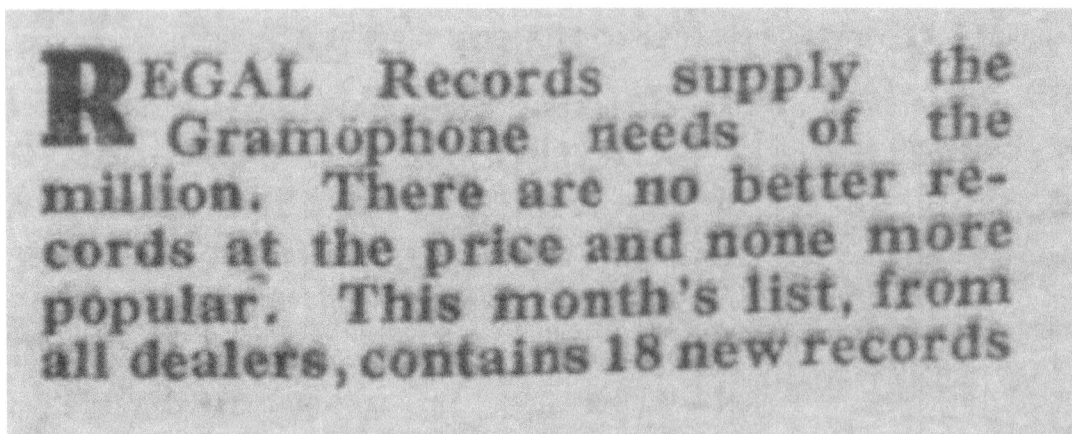

REGAL Records supply the Gramophone needs of the million. There are no better records at the price and none more popular. This month's list, from all dealers, contains 18 new records

(Image credit: The Daily Record.)

Lots of fingers in lots of pies, but Samuel wasn't finished yet. Between Rothesay, Glasgow and Stranraer, he was proprietor and managing director of several cinemas, a chain of photography studios, a freelance electrical engineering business, a property rental business, and a music agency and shop. Then, with his son, Victor, he set up his own car hire company at 159 Cathcart Road, Glasgow, with a listing for 72 Bankhall Street as the house address. However, as this was Victor's home address, it appears that Samuel had put his son in charge of the company. Samuel's love of cars and driving was well known, but unfortunately for him, in 1928, he was charged with a motoring offence at Falkirk J. P. Court:

> *A Justice of the Peace Court was held at Falkirk on Thursday. The Justices on the bench were Councillors Murdoch and Flanagan. The following motorists were each fined £1 in respect of lighting offences: - Frederick R. Burnette, 72 Bankhall Street, Govanhill, Glasgow.*
> (The Falkirk Herald 29 December 1928)

Samuel was the one charged, but it was Victor's address that was given. Two years later, Victor himself was up in the same court on a motoring charge relating to a parking offence.

Even with the costs of running so many businesses, Samuel must have had a reasonable annual income, allowing himself and Emily to live comfortably at their house on Hamilton Drive. However, they began to spend more time in Rothesay. Samuel was still the landlord of two dwelling houses, and by 1935, Emily and Samuel were living on the premises with the tenants at 31 Ardbeg Road, Rothesay, and they were still living there as late as 1940. However, as with many things in Samuel's life, this was not straightforward, and the Rothesay property is confusing. Samuel and Emily are known to have lived at Rosemount Cottage. But Rosemount Cottage doesn't appear on any Valuation Rolls until 1941, when it shows Emily living on her own as a widow at the property. Rosemount Cottage is a substantially sized house located directly behind the property at 31 Ardbeg Road. So, it is impossible to say exactly when Samuel and Emily moved into Rosemount Cottage and for how long they lived there before Samuel's death in 1940.

CHAPTER SIXTEEN

THE MYSTIC TWELVE

(Mystic Twelve badge, image credit: Magic Circle Archives.)

With Samuel and Emily settled comfortably into city life in Glasgow and with all the businesses secure, Samuel's career was well and truly established. He was held in high regard by his contemporaries within the business and entertainment communities. But as was the way with Samuel, this wasn't enough, and he looked for something else to fulfil his life. It was only natural that he would have looked back on his early career as a performer with affection. He must have had so many fond memories of performing as Professor Burnette, and he no doubt missed the attention of a live audience, no matter how successful his life in Scotland had become. So, Samuel went back to his first love, which was Magic. In 1920, Samuel set up a secret society of magicians called The Mystic Twelve with himself as president. The society only had twelve members at any given time, and potential members had to wait until somebody died or resigned from the society. The club's motto was "Fraternity, Fidelity and Progress." Club members even had a unique badge: a clock face with the letters MYSTIC TWELVE instead of numerals. An original badge can be seen at The Magic Circle H.Q. Museum in London. The Mystic Twelve met on the first Sunday of the month at Samuel's house at Hamilton Drive. Samuel went to great lengths to keep the society as secretive as possible, adding to its mystery and exclusiveness. Before each meeting, all members were sent a playing card in the post and had to present this card to gain entry to the meeting room. Samuel even went to the trouble of having his butler act as a guard stationed outside the room. He was given the title "Tyler," a word which seems to have its origins in old English, meaning "doorkeeper of the inn". At each meeting, members were required to perform an original trick or illusion to the assembled company. At one such meeting, Samuel performed his "Talking Skull" trick. Members were encouraged to ask the skull questions and await the reply from the skull's mouth. I can almost picture the scene. Knowing Samuel's flair for mystery and enchantment, what sort of ambience within the room did he create? Would there have been heavy drapes and low candlelight, with atmospheric music on the gramophone? It would be inappropriate to give away how the trick worked, but suffice it to say that Samuel wasn't averse to lifting a few floorboards and drilling a few holes in the walls of his house!

XII. Pres. F. R. Burnette. VI. Vice-Pres. C. Dacre.
I. Bro. N. L. Morkill. II. Past Bro. H Vernon.
III. Bro. T. J. Anderson. IV. Bro P. J. Smith.
V. Bro. De Vega. VII Bro. W. Dale.
VIII. Bro. J. Ramsey. IX. Bro. R. Armour.
X. Bro. Chris van Bern. XI. Bro. Oswald Williams.

(1927 Mystic Twelve members, image credit: Peter Lane collection.)

The original members were: *Frederick Rendell Burnette, President; William Jeffrey, Vice President, Nelson Lyford, Secretary, Ernardo Veneri, Charles Dacre, T.J Anderson, James Bel, J Loudon Palmer, Fred J. Smith, Harry F. Ashton, Harry Vernon, and Allan Peterson.*

It has been impossible to find out about every original member because I suspect that some of them were simply friends or acquaintances of Samuel.

William Jeffrey, Vice President, was a timber merchant from Glasgow and allegedly a friend of the Great Houdini. Houdini visited Glasgow in 1920, appearing at the Coliseum and Pavilion theatres, so is it possible that Samuel met Houdini? William Jeffrey was president of The Glasgow Society of Magicians, which was in existence from 1919 until 1924. It is not clear how long William Jeffrey was a member of the Mystic Twelve. Not only was he a conjurer, but also a spiritualist. In 1919, The Truth magazine published an article in which he was reported to have challenged Nevil Maskelyne to investigate phenomena that he considered to demonstrate the existence of intelligent unseen powers. In 1921, an article appeared in which Mr Jeffrey explained his belief in spiritualism:

> *On Tuesday evening an intensely interesting lecture entitled "Truths about Spiritualism" was given to the members of the Milngavie Social Union by Mr William Jeffrey, President of the Glasgow Society of Magicians… Mr Jeffrey was a man who had an ardent belief in spiritualism… Mr Jeffrey said that before he showed the slides of spirits or super normal pictures of some of their friends who had passed into the great beyond, he would just like to tell them why he became a spiritualist. He had been interested in conjuring since he was a boy. He had convinced many conjurers and illusionists as to the possibilities of getting in touch with those friends which many of them thought were dead and lying in the grave until that great day of resurrection.* (Glasgow Herald 18 November 1921)

William Jeffrey is mentioned twice in Sir Arthur Conan Doyle's History of Spiritualism, a collection of essays in two volumes published in 1926.

Nelson Lyford, Secretary, was born Nelson Morkhill, who in 1923 was Scout Commissioner for Glasgow. He performed around Scotland at organised events for children and adults of all ages and occasionally would give lectures on magic and conjuring to adult societies.

Ernardo Veneri was born in Reggiolo, Italy and became an N.C.O. in the 17th Regiment of Garibaldi's Volunteers or "Red Shirts" and was part of the Tyrol campaign of 1866. Because of his musical talent, he became a bandmaster in the army. When he was about 30, he came to England. He visited Bath, Samuel's hometown and performed there many times during the winter seasons. He even lived in Bath for several years, so it is highly likely that he and Samuel first crossed paths there. He was even a member of the Bath Lodge of the Royal Antediluvian Order of Buffaloes, one of the largest fraternal orders in the country. As well as an accomplished musician, he was also a very gifted conjurer. In later life, he was a member of the Scottish Orchestra in Glasgow for 13 years and was a regular player with the Pier Orchestra in Llandudno. He was still performing his conjuring act in his late 70's. He was buried in his Garibaldi red shirt, according to his last wishes.

Charles Dacre was a Glasgow conjurer and ventriloquist who performed at social groups and concerts. In 1924, he appeared at a New Year concert at Carluke town hall, performing his novel and humorous sleight-of-hand experiments.

J. Louden Palmer had been a member of the Universal Society of Magicians, based in Glasgow, between 1917 and 1918. In 1910, he appeared in Kirkcaldy at the Adam Smith Hall as a ventriloquist. In 1912, he appeared as a ventriloquist, sleight-of-hand artiste and musical humourist at organised Kirkcaldy Corporation Concerts. In 1930, he appeared at Jedburgh public hall in an entertainment for children as a ventriloquist and magician. During the show, he performed tricks with handkerchiefs, cards, dice and eggs.

Fred J. Smith was a founder member of the Scottish Conjurers' Association, the fourth magic society to be established in Glasgow, which still exists today. Fred's daughter, Miss Alice Maclay, was at one time the only female magician in Europe, and during WWII, she entertained troops all over Scotland.

Harry F Ashton was born in Gateshead into a family with a music hall background. He began his career selling theatre programmes in a northern theatre. He became the manager of the theatre before acting as manager to many travelling companies. After moving to Glasgow, he worked for Howard and Wyndham as assistant manager of the Royal Theatre, Glasgow, in 1906. In 1910, he became the manager of the Lyceum Theatre, Edinburgh, before moving back to Glasgow to manage the Theatre Royal. He stayed there until 1928 when he moved back to Edinburgh for a year. From 1929 to 1951, he was manager at the King's Theatre, Glasgow. During WWI, he produced many benefit concerts and shows for the troops and entertainment for wounded soldiers. Harry also served as president of the Musical Artistes Benevolent Fund.

Harry Vernon seems to have begun his stage career as a conjurer, ventriloquist and all-round entertainer. He performed around the Glasgow area, but he also had a connection to Bath. In 1914, while living in Philip Street, Bath, he advertised himself as a conjurer, ventriloquist and versatile entertainer for children's parties, bazaars, at homes and concerts. In the 1920s, he released songs for Regal Records (Samuel was an agent for this company). Vernon played the London circuit as well before returning to Bath for the Christmas Season in 1932. He advertised himself as a popular society entertainer who offered the most up-to-date novelties in conjuring, ventriloquism, sleight of hand and marionettes.

Allan Peterson had belonged to the same society as J Louden Palmer, the Universal Society of Magicians, from 1917 to 1918 in Glasgow. He then joined the Glasgow Society of Magicians, which ran from 1918 until 1924. He was a performing ventriloquist in the Glasgow area, toured with his Punch and Judy act and even had a Punch and Judy radio show on a local Glasgow station.

MYSTIC TWELVE DISCUSS A PROBLEM

A problem in magic being discussed by members of the Mystic Twelve Brotherhood at their sixth anniversary dinner at Hamilton Drive, Glasgow, this week. They are all well-known "wizards."

(Mystic Twelve gathering 1926, Samuel holding the skull, image credit: Peter Lane collection.)

The Mystic Twelve was a great success and became well known with reports and articles appearing in various conjuring publications. Later members included De Vega, Chris van Bern, Oswald Williams, John Ramsey, James B Findlay, Stanley Marne, Drew Masters, Richard Armour, and George McKenzie.

De Vega (real name Alex M Stewart) was a qualified physiotherapist who began his magic career as an escape artist and a skilled magician who invented many of his own legerdemain tricks. He was also an artist and photographer. He wrote many articles for various publications, was the author of numerous books and co-wrote "Whirlwind of Wizardry" with Chris van Bern. He became a pyrotechnic expert and was responsible for many of the large outdoor firework displays around the west coast of Scotland. He ran his fireworks business, Stewarts Displays, from Sword Street in Dennistoun, Glasgow. He was a friend of Harry Houdini and helped Houdini investigate the "spirit photographs" produced by the Derby Circle. While Houdini wanted to believe in communication with the spirits, he was determined to expose fraudulent mediums and their fakery. This led to Houdini publishing his book, "A Magician Among The Spirits," exposing such trickery. In the book, he pays thanks to De Vega: *"I would like to say for the benefit of the reader that De Vega is a skilled magical entertainer; has invented a number of legerdemain feats; contributed a number of interesting articles to magical publications; is a skilled artist and a clever photographer. I was very fortunate in being able to secure a man of his ability for the investigation."* De Vega was a member of several Magic Societies, including the Glasgow Society of Magicians and a founding member of the Scottish Conjurers' Association. He was also responsible for designing the programmes for The Mystic Twelve's annual dinners.

Chris van Bern was often described as "the act that cannot be described." He was a master of the quick change, and his act was a mixture of magic and music. On the 1911 census, was is listed as an actor-comedian, and his wife as a character actress. Playbills advertised his act as a "Revusical, Musical Magical Mixture Laughs! Smiles! Gasps!" He was a member, vice president and president of numerous magic societies across the country.

Oswald Williams (not to be confused with Charles Oswald Williams, who also performed under this name) was a skilled magician. At the start of his career in 1906, The Walsall Advertiser described him as "a young Magician with a promising future who jumped into fame at his first appearance with his new sleight of hand tricks and mysterious scenes." He designed and made his own illusions and toured with his own company. In 1915, the Leeds Mercury described his musical fantasy "The House That Jack Built" as a triumph of the art of stage wizardry. He was often described as "England's Foremost Illusionist."

John Ramsey was a Scottish close-up magician who was often described as "a Magician's Magician" because he liked to trick fellow conjurers. In 1994, Professor Edwin Dawes presented "Lights and Sleights from Ayr," a celebration of the life of John Ramsey in his home town of Ayr.

James B Findlay was a Glaswegian magician and one of the founder members of the Scottish Conjurers' Association. He was also a magic historian, collector and author. In 1940, he appeared on stage in a Grand Concert given by Harry Lauder, and he was described as a "Master of Magic." During the war years, he appeared in fundraising concerts to raise money for Christmas boxes for the troops overseas.

Stanley Marne was a Glaswegian conjurer who performed at concert parties and private functions. In 1933, he performed at a Christmas concert for factory workers at an explosive factory in Linlithgow. He mystified his audience for a full 30 minutes with his new tricks and had the audience spellbound with his patter.

Drew Masters was a harmonica-playing magician. He was described as the "red-headed Wizard." Assisted by his wife in 1967, he won the British Ring Shield, which is considered one of the most prestigious awards in the country.

Richard Armour was a Scottish Magician and a founding member of the Scottish Conjurers' Association and twice served as president of the society. He was known as "Conjurer Dick." He compiled the "Magic of the Scottish Conjurers Association," which was published in 1945.

George McKenzie was an engineer who, in the 1920s, gave up his career to take up performing magic full time. He evidently spent two years with an illusionist called "Rameses, The Egyptian Wonderworker". During these years, McKenzie acquired new skills, knowledge and performing experience. He was a member of the Scottish Conjurers' Association and, shortly afterwards, set up his own magic dealer business from home. Initially, he issued a free magazine, which later became a subscription magazine known as Mac's Monthly. In the 1940s, he performed in the Glasgow area and was known as "The Uncanny Scot." He appeared in a series of variety concerts entitled, "Sunday Night at Seven," at the Port Glasgow Town Hall where he was the Compere, introducing each act with a humorous story as well as performing his unique conjuring tricks. These concerts were held on behalf of the provost's fund to entertain the armed forces.

(Image credit: Edwin Dawes collection.)

The Mystic Twelve held annual dinners for members and their wives, usually at the Charing Cross Hotel in Glasgow. However, the second-anniversary dinner was held at 15 India Street, the home of Vice-President William Jeffrey. The annual dinners were very much a lengthy affair, starting in the afternoon and carrying on well past midnight. The celebration would consist of a reception with tea, a whist drive, dinner, entertainment (provided by the twelve members), games, music, toasts and occasional dancing. Emily D'Arc occasionally provided part of the entertainment as well with her marionettes. In 1924, Samuel was elected honorary president of the Scottish Conjurers' Association. After his death in 1940, there were only ever eleven members in the society as a mark of respect. The Mystic Twelve continued until 1960.

(The Mystic Twelve, Samuel far right, image credit: Margaret Murray.)

CHAPTER SEVENTEEN

AN AIR CRASH

This story of an air crash doesn't involve Samuel directly. However, this incident was widely reported in local and national newspapers, and it is more than likely that he would have read about it.

In January 1938, an aeroplane flying from Renfrew to Campbeltown to deliver film reels to the Picture House, crashed. The aircraft was a Spartan Cruiser III, which was operated by Northern and Scottish Airways. It regularly flew the Glasgow - Campbeltown – Islay route. That weekend, the west coast had been battered by gale force winds. On Friday 14th, the aircraft left Renfrew at 4.30 pm to deliver the cinema reels to the Picture House for that evening's showing. On board were Captain McGeevor the Pilot, and Officer Hughs the Wireless Operator. Luckily there were no passengers aboard the flight. At 5.13 pm news was received in Campbeltown by James McGeachy, superintendent of Campbeltown Airport, that the Pilot had been forced to turn back when over Pladda, an island off the south coast of Arran. The plane failed to return to Renfrew Airport. A widespread search over the Clyde, the Ayrshire and Renfrew coast was undertaken by the Troon and Girvan Lifeboats. Flares were lit at the landing strip at Prestwick R.A.F Training School and Police Forces from Ayrshire and Renfrewshire patrolled the coastal roads. Unfortunately, due to a malfunctioning altimeter, the Pilot believed he had gained enough height to clear the North Ayrshire hills before beginning his descent into the Airport. The wireless equipment had also failed which meant the Pilot was unable to radio for help or send a distress call. A few minutes after six o' clock, both the Pilot and the Wireless Operator had an amazing escape when the Pilot made a forced landing, the plane crashing in the in the darkness in the hills behind Largs. Both men were thrown clear of the wreckage, uninjured! Being completely lost in the darkness, the two men detached the compass from the plane and used it to guide themselves down the hillside, heading in a westerly direction which would eventually bring them to the shore side. After wandering in the dark and rain for two hours, the two men arrived exhausted at the Hills Hotel. The manager, Mrs Ramsay supplied the men with dry clothes and food. After their dramatic escape, Captain McGeevor reported that he had turned back because of the bad weather and made a forced landing near Largs after the wireless equipment had broken down and the under – carriage had been torn off. He and the wireless operator were unhurt but the plane was damaged. An official at the aerodrome said, "We almost collapsed when Captain McGeevor came on the phone. We could scarcely believe our ears when we heard him speaking." Meanwhile back in Campbeltown, apart from a few broken roof slates and local flooding, the town escaped the worst of the weekend gales.
(Campbeltown Courier 8 January 1938)

On a final note: As a result of the crash, the Picture House was closed on the Friday night – only the second time in its history that it had closed. The first time had been during the coal strike in 1926 when a film failed to turn up in time for a showing. And the film that never made it to Campbeltown in 1938? It was an American gangster movie, "Bullets or Ballots", starring Humphrey Bogart and Edward G Robinson.
The remains of the aircraft's fuselage are on display at the National Museum of Flight at East Fortune.

CHAPTER EIGHTEEN
JESSIE ROSE

What became of Jessie Rose, the wife that Samuel left behind in London? She was one of six children born in Bath to Ellen Alford and William Cottle. Her father's first occupation was a lamplighter, like his father before him. He later became a house painter.

By 1881, Jessie Rose's parents appeared to have been living separate lives, and the family was scattered. Her father was in lodgings in Portishead, and her mother was a domestic servant in Grosvenor House in Bath. At the same time, Jessie Rose and three of her siblings, George William, Ellen Elizabeth and Emily, had moved to London, where three of them were in domestic service. Jessie Rose as a Nursemaid, George William as a butler, Emily as a kitchen maid and Ellen Elizabeth was a dressmaker living in lodgings. Their youngest sibling, Henry, aged 10, had been left back in Bath, living as a Lodger with Thomas and Louisa Cardwell. Henry eventually arrived in London, becoming a baker then a house painter like his father. Jessie Rose's mother eventually moved to London and later shared a house with her son, George William. She became a nurse while George William continued to work in service. Something serious must have happened to cause the separation in the marriage because Jessie Rose's father ended up a Pauper in Bath Union Workhouse.

Samuel and Jessie Rose had married in St Peter's Parish Church, Twerton, Somerset, on 9 January 1884. They had eight children in total, although three died in infancy. Jessie Rose and Samuel began married life at 2 Kingsmead Terrace in Bath, and Jessie Rose travelled with Samuel some of the time. In 1891, she was in lodgings together with Samuel and their eldest daughter in Bristol. Samuel was performing as a ventriloquist at the time. But, as the family grew, Jessie Rose spent most of her time in Bath, bringing up the children and, at some point, moved from Kingsmead Terrace to Kingsmead Street. By 1900, two daughters, Hettie and Marie, had died, leaving Jessie Rose with five children to care for. The move to London was imminent, but Samuel wasn't the only one on the road performing around the country. Jessie Rose had begun her own stage career under the name Jessie Burnette rather than Rendell.

In January 1900, she appeared on stage at the Marylebone Music Hall. In March, she was part of a variety act in a music hall on Hackney Road. In October, she appeared at Leeds Varieties Music Hall, where her performance was described as above average. The following month, she was performing at the Empire Palace in Sheffield. In January 1901, Jessie Rose was on the London stage, appearing twice nightly at Foresters' Palace of Varieties, a music hall in Mile End. She was part of Will Godwin & Co's production, "A Rogue's Reward." A week later, she was part of Percy Murry's company in "The King's Jester" at The New South London Palace of Varieties on London Road. In June of the same year, Jessie appeared at the Hammersmith Palais singing and dancing:

> *Miss Jessie Burnette sings, "I'm a Bridesmaid," and after this, she submits a dance that may be said to ably support her vocalism."*
> (London and Provincial Entr'acte, 1 June 1901)

In July 1902, Jessie Rose appeared at The London Music Hall, Shoreditch. It was an enormous venue with a seating capacity of just over 2,300. Like most music halls of the time, the programme would change each week, and performers would be expected to perform every evening, including a Saturday matinee. In 1903, she was described as "a comedienne and dancer of no mean ability" when she appeared at the Camberwell Palace.

Did Samuel and Jessie Rose juggle and share the childminding duties between them to allow Jessie Rose to pursue her stage career, or were the children left with someone else entirely? In 1891, when Samuel was in Bristol, and Jessie Rose was with him in lodgings, they had taken their eldest daughter with them, but not their son Victor or their other daughter Grace Mona. Grace Mona, aged three months, had been left with the Penny family in Bath as a boarder. Why did Jessie Rose take to the stage in the first place? Had this always been her ambition? Did Samuel encourage her, and did his contacts in the industry help her establish her singing career? Or did Jessie Rose feel that she had to do something to bring in extra money and therefore decided to put her singing talents to good use?

Samuel had sold the waxworks at Upper Street by auction in March 1903, but what did he do with the money? The family continued to live there until August of that year, so perhaps the funds weren't released until then. Meanwhile, Jessie Rose struggled financially because Samuel was having an affair with Emily D'Arc, and he had left the marital home, even though Jessie Rose was pregnant. Things for Jessie Rose got so desperate that she could not look after herself or the children, so she took Samuel to court in November on a charge of desertion. By the time of the court appearance, Jessie Rose had given birth to their youngest son, Sam Redvers. In court, Jessie Rose told the judge how she had ended up in Wolverhampton workhouse because she couldn't survive on the £1 a week that Samuel was giving her. Jessie Rose told the judge that she didn't want the children. Instead, she wanted Samuel to have them because he didn't know them. Samuel said that he was fond of the children, and he agreed to take care of them.

What happened next after the court case is unclear. Did Samuel take all six children, or did he and Jessie Rose come to an arrangement? Between 1903 and 1906, there is very little documentation to tell what Samuel was doing until he moved to Scotland and opened his waxworks in Glasgow. Did he settle in Wales with his children at the D'Arc's family home? It is doubtful that Emily's mother would have approved of the situation or allowed it. Was he on the road with six children to look after, one of them a very young baby? Or did he return to Bath to be with his mother after the death of his father? The Probate document for his father's death shows Samuel as executor of his father's estate, and he is listed as Samuel John Rendell, photographer.

After the court case, she continued with her stage career, and in March 1904, she appeared in a variety show at the Granville Theatre of Varieties in Walham Green, London. Throughout 1906 and 1907, Jessie Rose performed in variety shows all around the country, including The Empire in Leeds, the Bordesley Palace in Birmingham and the Empire Theatre in Bradford. In addition, she appeared in theatres and music halls in Dublin, Belfast, Liverpool, Manchester, Birmingham, and Cardiff. She was described as a performer who danced neatly and was a pleasing comedienne, so it looks as if Jessie Rose was taking on more versatile roles and not just relying on her singing voice to make a living. In November 1906, she even travelled to Glasgow to appear at the Zoo Hippodrome, which had its own circus big top, roller skating rink and a theatre. Samuel was already established in Glasgow, but there is no evidence that they met up. In 1908, she was on the road, appearing in Sheffield, Halifax, Warrington, Dover and one performance at the Palace Theatre in her hometown of Bath.

The 1911 Census shows Jessie Rose still living in London at Ardleigh Road with her youngest daughter, Daisy May. She gave her occupation as a stage professional and singer and her status as married. In May of that year, Jessie Rose performed as a dancer, comedienne and vocalist at the Royal Hippodrome in Eastbourne, but then the trail goes cold in terms of her career as a singer. Before 1917, she and Daisy May moved to St Stephen's Street, Hounslow. By 1930, Jessie Rose was living on Fellows Road, sharing a property with two other women. The next few years are blank, so it is uncertain whether she stayed in London or not. But in 1937, Jessie Rose moved to Glasgow, where she lived with her eldest daughter, Jessie Emily, and her son-in-law at Windsor Street in Glasgow. She lived there until her death the following year. Jessie Rose died on 2 November 1938 at the Western Infirmary, Glasgow. On her death certificate, her given name is Jessie Rose Burnette (formerly Rendell). Her son, Victor Burnette, registered her death.

Samuel John Rendell, Cinema Proprietor, married to (1) Jessie Rose Cottle, (2) Emily D'Arc, died 10 June 1940, aged 79, at Rosemount Cottage, Rothesay.

The Buteman newspaper printed a heartfelt obituary a few days after Samuel's death, expressing the shock and sadness within the community at the loss of such a well-loved and much-respected Rothesay businessman. It gave an insight into his generosity through his charitable contributions of food parcels each Christmas to those in need and private monetary gifts to private individuals. A small mention was made of his passion for conjuring and magic, his role within the Scottish Society of Magicians, and how he was the founder and president of the Mystic Twelve. The article explained that because of Mr F R Burnette's promise to cater for all tastes and audiences, he had brought pleasure to cinema-goers for many years. The article states, " *he brought some of the most notable films it has ever seen to Rothesay. He brought to the de luxe screen many exceptional pictures off the beaten track simply because they were good films, although knowing full well that they were a shade too fine to win wide popular acclaim and attract big audiences, a gesture for which lovers of good cinema were properly grateful to him.* " As a mark of respect, the cinema was closed for the three days following the funeral, after which it was business as usual with films booked for several months in advance.

For all his business interests over the years, Samuel did not die a particularly wealthy man. But he left enough to make sure that Emily D'Arc was looked after. She inherited the cottage in Rothesay and her pick of items from the house in Glasgow, including the "Singing Bird", which was an automaton bird operated by clockwork, a statement piece to be found in drawing rooms of the upper classes. There were no surprises in Samuel's last will and testament: a few small bequests to the trustees, his secretary and his manager, and his Wolseley motor car to his grandson. The remainder of the estate was divided between Emily and his children.

At the time of his death, Samuel was the sole owner of the Theatre de Luxe cinema in Rothesay, and he still owned shares in the Campbeltown Picture House and the Partick Picture House. Of all his cinemas, Campbeltown Picture House is the only one to have survived as a cinema and retained its name.

Samuel was a mover and shaker, a self-styled go-getter of his time, driven by ambition and hungry for success. Many of his decisions and plans were almost visionary, rooted in imagination with a touch of foresight and creativity. There must have been times when Samuel experienced despair and sadness, but his hope and determination overcame whatever adversity he faced. He was certainly clever and undoubtedly cunning, the Graveyard Monster episode being one example. Throughout his early career, he did travel to far off lands, namely London and Glasgow, seeking fortune and adventure, encountering some mysterious, colourful, and dubious characters along the way. His whole life was a giant quest. He took some wrong turns and made some disappointing decisions along the way. But he lived life to the fullest, with many moments of excitement and acts of daring-do. There was romance, too, and his love affair with Emily D'Arc was clearly the greatest passion in his life. However, his treatment of Jessie Rose was shameful and hardly the actions of a caring, honest, or honourable man. Samuel proved he was both hero and villain in different situations in his life, able to spin a tangled web of lies and half-truths to further his own interests.

And finally, like all good Fairy Tales, there was most definitely magic. Whether it was sleight-of-hand tricks for children in a schoolroom or the magic of moving pictures in his cinema palaces, magic was Samuel's first and most enduring love affair. He was the master of transformation, from a blacksmith's son to Professor Burnette, and his metamorphosis into Frederick Rendell Burnette, businessman and entrepreneur. Real life was Samuel's stage.

"...the soi-disant Magician must, in the first place, learn to believe in himself. When he steps upon the stage, he should, for the time being, persuade himself that his fictitious power is a reality."
(Professor Hoffmann, Modern Magic.)

And a final word from Samuel:

I have been in business since 1885. I have been pleasing and displeasing people ever since. I have lost money and made money. I have been cussed and discussed, knocked about, talked about, lied to, held up, flattered, robbed. I have lent money to friends. I HAVE LOST MY FRIENDS. The only reason I am staying in business is to see what the H——— will happen next.

For advice on above apply: {(Mr. B). De Luxe,
Rothesay,
Isle of Bute.

Acknowledgements

This book would not have been possible without the following people:

I am indebted to Professor Edwin Dawes for his support, encouragement, enthusiasm, and unstinting patience in answering my questions, sharing his knowledge of magic, magicians, and secret societies and generously allowing me to include images from his own personal collection. Thanks to Peter Lane, Magic Circle Executive Librarian Emeritus, who has kindly shared photographs and articles from his private collection and who located the Mystic Twelve badge from the Magic Circle archive. Enormous thanks to Iain Armstrong, Margaret Murray and Ron Armstrong, descendants of Samuel John Burnette, who generously shared family ephemera, documents, and photographs. Grateful thanks to Ray Clitheroe and Noelle Fitzgerald, descendants of the D'Arc family, who happily shared information and family secrets with me and allowed me access to Jane D'Arc's letter. Huge thanks to Chris Doak, architect, whose knowledge of Glasgow cinemas was invaluable and for his generosity in allowing me to use his drawings. Thanks to Morag Cross, a researcher, who provided me with information on the history of Glasgow's early roller rinks. Thanks to Gordon Sydney, historian of Clyde F.C. who searched out articles from his archives. Enormous thanks to June Budd and Margaret Taylor, descendants of Frank Lind, for supplying information, articles, and photographs. Special thanks to Ellen Mainwood, manager at Campbeltown Picture House, for her help and support. Grateful thanks to Jean McMillan, archivist at Bute Museum, for seeking out Rothesay articles and photographs. Grateful thanks to Bruce Peter, Professor of Design History, for his advice and permission to use an image from his collection. Thanks to Richard Stenlake, publisher, for allowing me to include his photo of Campbeltown Picture House. Thanks to Tony Wilson, photographer and archivist, for his encouragement and advice. Thanks to Marian Pallister, author, who generously shared her time, expertise, advice and encouragement. Thanks to the editor of the Oban Times, who allowed me to use images and articles from the Campbeltown Courier. Thanks to the Daily Record, who allowed me to use adverts from their publications. Thanks to The Herald, who gave permission to transcribe and use articles. Thank you to Judith Bowers of the Britannia Panopticon Music Hall, who gave permission to quote parts of the prospectus from Pickard's Papers collection. Thanks to JPIMedia for allowing me to transcribe articles from various publications. A special mention and thanks must go to Robin Patel, historian and curator who first encouraged me to tell F R Burnette's story.

This book has taken years of research, and I found the writing process lengthy and difficult. I am fortunate to have so many supportive friends and family who have encouraged and supported me every step of the way. Many times, I wanted to give up, but my husband and daughter convinced me to keep going because they believed in me. Derek and Alexandra, you are my strength and my inspiration.

Printed in Great Britain
by Amazon